T0208388

Hospice, Grief, and Life Thereafter

WITH HEARTFELT GRATITUDE TO GOD

DR. SHERRI LYNN BURES

Scripture quotations marked KJV are from the Holy Bible, King James Version
(Authorized Version). First published in 1611. Quoted from the KJV Classic
Reference Bible, Copyright © 1983 by The Zondervan Corporation.

Order this book online at www.trafford.com
or email orders@trafford.com

Most Trafford titles are also available at major online book retailers.

Print information available on the last page.

ISBN: 978-1-4907-6626-3 (sc)
ISBN: 978-1-4907-6627-0 (hc)
ISBN: 978-1-4907-6630-0 (e)

Library of Congress Control Number: 2015917076

Trafford rev. 10/22/2015

 www.trafford.com
North America & international
toll-free: 1 888 232 4444 (USA & Canada)
fax: 812 355 4082

Ask the voice of God to come to you: Then listen, write, and humbly thank Him with your gratitude.

Written through the Grace of God.

Dedication

This is dedicated to God the Father, God the Son, and God the Holy Spirit ever present with me, at all times, clearly my inspiration for this book, writing, sharing, and living.

To Saint Theresa, Thank-you for channeling information to me. She said to me in my dream, "Peace, Joy, Acceptance...the pain that we carry in our heart, our bosom, is not meant to be lasting, because we never lose the soul that is eternal...the connection is soul..."

To all the Saints...The Blessed Virgin Mary, Mary Magdalene, Saint Joseph, Saint Theresa, St. Michael, St. Raphael, my Masters, Guides, Archangels, and Angels,

To my #1 Soldier who continues to watch over me, your wisdom and kind words from the afterlife continue to shine in my life I lead today. May God protect us both and all we hold dear in this world and in the next...And to all your fellow service men and women who served alongside you during the Vietnam War may I personally say, "Welcome Home".

To my four children: Paul. Suzy, Robert, and Mickey whom I believe as a mother, I have been blessed by God himself. I love each and every one of you from the bottom of my heart. You are the finest representatives of God's love I could have ever wished for.

To Pastor Julian Graham, you are a dear friend who showed love and hope always. Thank you for being the first person to call me, because you just knew what had occurred. The Lord told you. To Linda your lovely wife who was a true friend to both of us. God Bless both of you and your lovely family.

To my dear friend Marina who understood that miracles happen both by life and by death, and it is up to us to accept the Will of God. She has always showed unconditional love to all people that have asked for her prayers. With sincere gratitude I know God has blessed you Marina by being a living testament that angels are on Earth.

To my dear cousin Terry who stood by my side through the entire hospice situation. Thank you very much. To my cousin Colin your kind words gave me hope that I could survive. I will always remember you reached out to me and made sure I knew my family loved me and needed me.

To the one whom I will always wish the finest of God's infinite grace and wisdom, who doesn't have to say a word, yet feels in his heart I will always love him.

To everyone who one day will have to bare this torture. I truly wish you the peace and love that only Our Savior Jesus Christ of Nazareth can give to us. May God always watch over you with His Fatherly Grace. May the Holy Spirit guide every action you go through and give you the wisdom to do it.

Contents

Dedication vii
Introduction to Hospice, Grief, and Life Thereafter xi

Chapter 1   The Diagnosis.. 1
Chapter 2   Hospice-Support For Comfort 29
Chapter 3   Ideas To Help Through Hospice 95
Chapter 4   Spiritual Help During Hospice 201
Chapter 5   The End, When Death Arrives............................... 267
Chapter 6   Grief.. 291
Chapter 7   God's Help Through Prayer 333
Chapter 8   After Life In Heaven 365
Chapter 9   Recovering By Learning To Live Again And
             Memorials To Our Loved Ones 413
Chapter 10   Prayers.. 475

Introduction to Hospice, Grief, and Life Thereafter

I experienced first hand life in a hospice center for six months with my dearest man. Grief and Life after losing him followed. It was the best of times and it shall always remain the best of times. I loved him with unconditional love. Hopefully I can give an insiders look toward the emotional side of this experience. This is taken from my notes and experiences, not his. To go through this with someone does take a toll, perhaps more than we can imagine. What good came from this is only that I might be able to help someone else, cope. For isn't that all that is important in this world, but to help others. One last remark about my dearest, he looks down from heaven with a beautiful smile on his face, knowing that I made it and with all the knowledge I acquired, might be able to help someone else.

This book was written through my experience from a caring, devoted point of view of always holding him first; as he held my feelings first as well. I wrote this to help both the patient and caregiver. It is written with total love toward God, because that is how I live my life. The book has poetry intermixed with writing. The poems may be used to speak to the patient or the caregiver. I wrote this book through my heart rather than the in and out details of living in a hospice facility.

I was told very clear by God on May 13, 2011 on Topsail Beach, North Carolina while I was walking on the beach enjoying the ocean; that I would write a book, "And you shall write, so others may live". May each of us in whatever way possible help those that need our help doing this in the name of the One who created us all, Our Lord and Savior Jesus Christ of Nazareth.

And I Write

And I write,
Hoping that these words console someone,
It is not me,
Words to me are a therapy,
A retreat,
    A release of anxieties,
    Built up frustrations,
Jumping in black and blue ink,
Expressions of deep grief,
Why's,
Even though why's can never be explained,
I try as hard as I can,
    To understand,
The Almighty's plan,
I was brought up with faith,
I feel I have tremendous faith,
Yet, I am human,
I am living a human existence,
And pain is not foreign to that existence,
It is real,
It is horribly real,
No education,
    No religious training,
    Can teach you,
Take your hurt away,
Only living through this can,
Will it ever leave,
I do not know,
I cannot tell at this moment,
I just try,
With my beautiful pen,
And my words that ramble,
I try,
I do try...
SLB

I love you.

Chapter 1
The Diagnosis

My Heavenly Father,
Thank you for my great love of Your Son Jesus,
Thank you for Jesus to always love all of us,
May we all receive blessings for those we love,
May Jesus comfort you, as your belief in Him becomes very strong,
Blessings sent to this beautiful world we live in.
Amen.
SLB

The words you dare not hear. Please don't let me hear them, perhaps if I smile I won't understand a word, but you do. And whether you pretend or not, you ultimately have to face the news. This is the present time when everything comes together, the diagnosis is given. You accept it with Grace. Grace. Fill it with your whole body; bathe in the Grace that only God can give. Ask God to allow your body to have Grace. A beautiful word, but so powerful, a message, the Grace of God. Pray it, feel it, and fill yourself with the Grace of God.

Life has a way of changing quickly. After you hear the diagnosis, you become grateful, for what you have. So grateful, you never fully understand until you are in that predicament. Know when that happens, you will be fine, adjust your will, with the help of the Lord.

Remember When

Remember when life was simple,
Remember when life was good,
Health was our haven,
Happiness lived in our home,
Laughter surrounded us,
Laughter made our day,
Peace and serenity followed us,
Each and every day...
SLB

Life totally changes with a diagnosis of possible mortality. The time you hear the words kick off a signal to live and fight. It can sometimes be a gift as in finding Jesus Christ and in becoming a better person in the long haul. Numbness and total "zombie ness" occur shortly after the diagnosis, if you are reading these words instead of going through it, I hope this will help. Numbness which is unexplainable occurs after the diagnosis. You go about your business, but you are empty inside. Even for someone who lives in God daily, it somehow surfaces. It is unbearable to wait for it to fade. Sometimes you feel you can't even look at people, can't make it across the room, and tears are a constant reminder. You ask yourself, I thought prayer. Well it is prayer. But-deeper than you thought to go. Allow yourself to go deep as deep as you possibly can.

Relief will come. It will. It may take time, but allow the peace of God to help. It is truly amazing. You may have your up and down moments, realize you are human. Remain constant in your devotion. Thank God when you are feeling better, ask Him to soothe away the numbness. Ask Him to fill you with the tasks to ease the way. Surely this will help. A strong relationship with God is so powerful, it becomes beautiful, awesome. The power of God heals, creates miracles (small or large), and gives us the strength to get through our days, and the hope for many tomorrows...

People sometimes volunteer more, give of themselves to others and what they give they get it back twice fold. They learn to appreciate what they have, the gifts God has given to them, and they reach out and help those less fortunate than them. Volunteering is a two-fold both parties are satisfied, you can get great joy from the act of volunteering. When you walk in the path of those you help, your journey does not seem so severe. After volunteering in New Orleans several years after Katrina hit, I still felt my problems and those of everyone around me could never compare to what devastation the French Quarter, the 9th Parish witnessed, and I knew my problems and those that I love would be small to this. God truly had many to handle after Katrina.

My Very Best At This Time

My very best at this time,
Forever into the universe of our eternity,
May the good Lord always watch over you and
    keep you,
May He bless every person you are concerned over,
Ever cared about, or ever will care about in the future,
And may everyone's blessings be fulfilled.
Amen.
SLB

Life is not predictable and bad news may strike at anytime. You may experience an accident changing the course of your day. Nothing is certain. I do hope that some of the poetry I have written may give you comfort whether it be as a patient or from the care-givers perspective.

There Has Been A Scare

I love you, it's true, there has been a scare,
Terrifying both of us, because we deeply care...
Understanding the dynamics of what you said,
Trying to advise, of all that I've read...
My God, what I would give to make you well,
Anything they would ask of me, I'd tell...
Time is our most precious commodity, hon,
I'm asking your mother to come, bless her son...
Angels I've beckoned, to help my man at last,
I've felt Jesus surround me, as in my past...
But our deepest of faith, the lessons we shall learn,
Oh, but Lord I need him with me, I yearn...
Peace and my deepest love, I'll send to your heart,
Sickness in my sweetheart, will not make us part...
I wish I could be with you, I'll hold out my hand,
Together, forever and one day, we will stand...
You'll love me, as much as I love you,
Someday my love, yes, darling, let's say, I do...
SLB

The treatments are a series of ups and downs. When the nurse calls and gives the news, remember the patient is the one affected. They learn to live between the treatments. Live in the moment. Enjoy life as best as you can. Absorb everything you can. Look at the beauty in everything that God gives us. They hear numbers, but always remember the number to hear is hope. Sometimes the patient is even trying to help the support person. They want to spare them the same pain they are going through. When the prognosis is bad it can become a rough decision whether to take time off from treatments to live. If that be the case, live. Have fun and do not worry. Live as though you have no problems. Time we spend with loved ones is time given to us from God. Enjoy this time. Enjoy the fact you had time with them and Live.

I was walking outside in Jacksonville alongside the river on Easter evening and noticed a beautiful cross over the hospital. It was as if a gift had been given to us from God.

Beautiful Cross In The Sky

Beautiful cross in the sky,
    I pray to you, please bless my guy...
    I have seen your beauty by the sea,
    Awakening up peacefulness inside of me...
Beautiful cross in the sky,
    Asking me to absorb your essence with my eye...
    I feel your force all around,
    The waves splashing with their beautiful sound...
Beautiful cross in the sky,
    I come to admire you, my, oh my...
    You sit beside this mighty river,
    I pray to my Lord, it sends me a shiver...
Beautiful cross in the sky,
    Thinking of creation, pondering how and why...
    You've given me strength when I sat to look,
    Inspiring to read your words in the Holy Book...
Beautiful cross in the sky,
    Always I hope to remember you, before I must
    say bye...
    For tonight, I shall go, and not return,
    But pray to God and always I shall learn...
SLB

Be grateful for all of life's lessons that being the case I am very grateful I was the one chosen to help him through this process. When both of you can look at each other and thank the Lord you have that person to be with you supporting you through thick and thin, you are truly blessed. It is easier when two people can share the journey.

Sometimes the best decision you can make is to live your life the very best that you can with the diagnosis. Put quality into your life. Exercise considered fun can give you more strength enabling your body to fight harder. Please be aware there are times you may not want to get up. Your body is so tired you desperately don't want to talk, don't want to go on. There are times you barely make it, not knowing your tomorrow. How do you tell those closest to you, you don't care, you want to sleep, you are tired beyond. You might hurt their feelings. They won't understand and then perhaps not call. What good would that do, the struggles are endless, the ups and downs, the time management problems. How do you spend your days, when you don't know how many you have left? Remember, known of us know that answer. Only God knows the fact. Be ready for your next battle stay physically strong, emotionally strong, and spiritually strong and in that sense you are where you should be. Thank God he is giving you those options to do that.

Is it truly one person's fight or those of the entire family. It is an individuals' choice. I saw from a parents' perspective it was difficult at times to discuss it with children. Protecting their feelings was an important choice. People say they want you to share. The cold hard facts of how horrible and tough some days were would frighten our loved ones, and deciding to keep silent and inward was not simply a choice but an act of love. Do not judge those that are in such pain, for we do not know how we would react given what they have dealt with. It all boils down to the Ying/Yang situation of trying to protect the ones you love verses the fact that telling your concerns releases stress, and that is a blessing.

During treatments be aware if you begin to feel a little sick or question something. Call your professional and get an examination. Fevers can occur quickly changing your prognosis, be aware that your body is dealing with a lot, so use caution and remember it is you going through the treatments not someone else, take care of yourself.

After the diagnosis sets in, remember you are on God's time. Praise God give him thanks for every blessing He gives to you. Your soul will grow with each and every problem and you will always be exactly where you are supposed to be in your lifetime. Keep God number one in your life, ask for a healing, and use every opportunity wisely.

Understand and let God handle your life, and everything will be as it was meant to be. Patience and Faith in God gives you strength, and Love is a constant, that never changes, Believe.

Pain and suffering are words you might think of when you hear the diagnosis, but life isn't all bad. With pain you learn to live each day, whatever God gives you. Suffering is erased in life's most beautiful moments-the birth of a grandchild, birthdays, Christmas. God blesses us with life-good or bad it is life.

The Lord Sent You To Me

The Lord sent you to me from up above,
   To show me an emotion, we'll call it love...
I've never experienced such feelings I share with you
   today,
   Words can never express what I want to say...
You've enriched all my senses, I cannot ask for more,
   My emotions they are satisfied, as none has been
   before...
You understand me totally, so accepting and so true,
   My love, no one else exists for me, only you...
SLB

Let us hope you, or your loved one is never faced with the diagnosis. But, if you are, face it head on. Face it with Grace. Listen, be polite, ask God to stop your tears, and then quietly when no one is around, you have my permission to crash. Cry, cry with all your heart and soul, get it out of your system. Talk to anyone that will listen to all your pain. And tell whoever will listen how you feel. Be honest, have a solid plan of action. First accept it, know the reality of the situation. And once you have accepted it, really accepted the true reality; then only then Pray. Pray and Hope for the best. Hope for your Miracle. Give it to God.

Dream I Shall, As I Sit Here By The River

Dream I shall, as I sit here by the river,
　　Searching for answers not given,
Yet, I wait,
Hoping above all for one miracle in my lifetime,
Connecting to my Lord,
　　Here-such peace,
Yes, I have,
Near, in this river a cross on Easter,
I have seen beauty on Holy week,
I have seen the sacredness of knowing you while,
Now I seek, a miracle,
So I ask my Lord above.
　　For one person, one person, I ask,
　　And health be so fine,
　　Would make all our troubles unwind,
Peace and serenity from this hectic cycle,
　　And rest from all the burdens he has,
That is what my miracle entitles,
I ask the Lord above, to please consider,
　　If it is his will, that,
He will be grateful,
　　As I won't be sad,
For time is what we ask for...
SLB

The diagnosis must be handled head on. Listen to what is said and talk about it. Get angry, cry, talk some more. Talk to the one person that will allow you to cuss, yell, scream, and still love you in the morning. Let the person whose mortality decide. It is their journey. They want their independence. They will respect you more if you allow them to accept this. Remember, be kind. Loved ones have their own personal battles as well.

The hardest part of the diagnosis for the patient is to deal with it on their level and that of their family and significant other. Normally you are given the facts and there is no time of quiet meditation to sort this and process it out. After that if you are immediately thrown into projects such as bingo, people visiting, therapy, movies you may go inwards and say I need time to just think. Time becomes a problem, when everyone has control of your time but you. You may grow impatient with your partner due to over demanding demands. Perhaps crabby was never in the equation before. Time and quiet heal. God gave us the gift of time and quiet and to Him we should be grateful. Ask others to respect that. Absolute quiet and small talk to process all that you have to adjust to is very important.

And when this is said and done about your diagnosis, life has a way of working out. God's plan is revealed. We might not know what is best, but He knows. Give it to God. He will solve everything. He is the greatest healer in the universe. Have total faith in God. Let go and give it to God, and you never have to worry again. Peace, how beautiful peace can be. The peace that only the Creator can give us. Thank you God, and now I ask Him to bless all my troubles and yours as well.

God is the Healer. God is in charge. Whatever we want, whatever we or the doctors do with the best of intentions. God is the ultimate healer. We are all on the Lord's time, and no one knows when they will meet their maker.

You fear the diagnosis, and then you give your total submission to God. Is it easy? No it is the hardest job you will ever do. It is harder than labor, harder than the slaves in Egypt.

Yet it has to be done, all of the requests, prayers, promises all of them are carefully given to God. Significant people in your life, will try and try again, coming up with plan after plan, trying everything that can be tried, but only one knows the truth, and that is God.

When you surrender to God, a peace comes upon you. Knowing God has our best interests in mind. The best interests for everyone involved in the process. Difficult as it may be, when you feel the peace that comes from God, you know, you understand, it is real.

Faith heals. Believe and it shall be. Ask and it shall be given, seek and you shall find. Knock and it will be opened for you. Ask God, and then listen. God works in mysterious ways, be open to whatever comes your way, but also know, it was sent from above.

Give thanks, total for whatever God gives you that day, give Him thanks. Be grateful, so grateful, because blessings are a beautiful gift. Be humble unto the Lord, remember He is the Father, we are the child. Praise Him for the little things for when you add them up, they become the big. God is gracious, every day I am here, is truly a miracle, and I thank Him dearly.

Christ gives us divine healing through light and love. The unconditional love of God is very powerful. You feel it penetrate your body. Ask it to nourish your cells, rejuvenating each one for a healing that encompasses both emotional, physical, and spiritual. The happiness and joy you feel with Christ radiates outward, and it is contagious. Smile and you can give more pleasure to someone than a hundred dollar check. People communicating with people, socializing in this world is what our Creator intended. None of us want to be alone. We should not have to invite someone to a feeling of happiness, by providing them with the gift of a smile.

I believe through God only, a complete healing can occur. God is in charge. Doctors and nurses may do their best, but the hands of God placed upon a person, heals. God also uses the hands of doctors, nurses, and caregivers. We need to understand this and remember to be grateful and say thank you every moment we are pain free.

Remember God never gives us more than we can handle. We might think he does. He might be tempted to scream, 'God it's too much." But He knows, when life is too hard to handle, step outside. Yes, put your life on hold. Step away from it. Breathe, drink a glass of water, touch the grass with your feet and renew yourself. Tell yourself I can do it. I can. When God really gives you too much to handle, and the pain is tormenting you, go inside. Totally go toward your soul, feel, and connect only with God. Pray for grace to fill your body and relief in some manner to come. Although none of us want others to suffer, it occurs. Just be there for the person, allowing the person to express what his feelings are, his pain. Offer support and of course love.

You as a human being, but a soul connected to God want to be a support system for this person. Sometimes all we can do is listen. Other times we just have to be there. Let your heart guide you, do not second judge yourself, and you will do as you were intended to do. I dedicate this last paragraph in this section, to the one who taught me beyond what I thought I could. Thank you my living angel...

You Are My Sunshine

You are my sunshine that brightens my every day,
    Always giving me love, strength, and support your
    own way...
You who awakened me to become a Light worker in
    this life,
    Praying for others ahead of myself, to end their
    strife...
Let your heart be always open to all that is,
    And your Spirit be ever so loving to His...
May the Lord Bless you and keep you; if it is God's will,
    I will be there also to love and care for my precious
    Bill...
SLB

Promises may be difficult for us to always keep. God promised all of us eternal life with Him if we believe. And that might be the best known promise. I have not kept all of my promises, but I was as sincere as I could be when I made them.

Promises, Promises

Promises I cannot always give you,
But hope and sincere well wishes I can,
Promises are not made to break,
But life gets out of hand,
Forcing us to contemplate,
Sincerity we truly meant,
Vanished with unexpected circumstances,
We might not have foreseen,
Promises may be of total trust,
And that I do give,
For as I was once told,
Do not promise many,
Promise but a few,
Be fervent and sincere,
With your full heart,
For God oversees our promises,
We are held accountable for pledging them,
So be discreet in what you promise,
And the one promise you do give,
Make that the promise you will keep,
The one you will remember in your heart,
The promise, your promise, this lifetime...
Today You Gave Me Your Promise

Today you gave me your promise,
The first you ever did pledge,
A promise to never forget you,
And caught me quite by surprise,
For never, I ever did imagine,
A promise you would give to me,
I do-yes so appreciate it,
It meant a lot to me,
You carried that through, from centuries past,
Your love that was promised, had a shattered past,
With knowledge, your freedom, you did attain,
And to me, a promise I will gain,
For love, it is mine, forever from you,
And I too, do promise, to never forget you,
For to promise, dare not take it lightly,
It is precious, give it just, do not ever let it break apart,
For our love, I am sure, will last with heart...
SLB

This is a side note for those who have been diagnosed from a caregiver point of view; we want to know the truth. It is far better to know what you are dealing with than to keep anything from us. Two people can handle things or the worst of news better than one. If you are the patient do not try to save that person from hurt. It is better to go through this life journey with someone than without. The truth is far better than avoidance and many other problems will stem up when you are masking the situation. Face it head on and with someone you trust.

Sometimes I Forget

Sometimes I forget, that your pain lingers on,
Sometimes I forget, all the fighting you've done,
For day to day problems they do come our way,
Solving them clutters our minds today,
So yes I don't dwell on this pain that you've had,
I focus on the present, the now, and I'm glad,
To bury all pain and problems from your past,
You'll be so free of it all at last,
Now on to the present and future let's go,
We've got a great future, I do think so,
Together we'll get through that awful pain you bare,
We'll make it through together, because I care...
SLB

The Serenity Prayer

God grant me the serenity to accept the things, I cannot
    change,
The courage to change the things I can,
and the wisdom to know the difference.
Amen.

My heart is by his side...
SLB

Chapter 2
Hospice-Support For Comfort

The word hospice rattles inside you. If you don't use the word, perhaps the situation might change. We took a tour of the hospice unit. The pleasantries didn't exist at that time. We were in an unknown world, questioning why we were chosen for a tour. We ultimately knew, but acceptance was far in the distance.

Later that same day he was transferred to hospice. What would hospice be like, enters your mind. Would he leave? Would he feel the sunshine on his face, questions rumble through your brain, yet neither of us showed our emotions. He entered as a gentleman and I as a lady.

Even though that is how I appeared to the outside world, I felt I was walking into a black mass. It was to be total fear of the unknown, the diagnosis, the outcome. Should we look left, should we look right? Should we look at the faces of the people, or just concentrate on what each of us had to deal with.

Smiles started appearing, laughter began, a joke, perhaps a gesture of friendship, and then without warning it happened, kindness. Fear was uplifted by kindness. Could this be true? Could the kindness of strangers take away the darkest moment, the black mass of fear, and the total fear of the diagnosis.

Suddenly God had given us a gift, a peace, and the word was kindness. From the kindness of strangers, who would eventually be friends, we had found peace. Fear was replaced by a smile, a message, a look and then magically as you can imagine we looked at others, we spoke, we cared about them. Life was better. Hospice became more of a family than a dark tunnel. And the realization that this could be positive, not negative became a reality.

Life was good. We had settled into the reality of the situation. When you are in an actual hospice home your food, laundry, and cleaning is done. The only responsibilities you have are to enjoy yourself. If the pain is under control you can experience many new things as I will discuss in the chapter, help with hospice. You don't know how good feels until you feel bad. Daily life and the hope of getting strong was very important in the hospice unit.

There are many people on the staff to be of assistance. There is a hospice program director who also gives counseling and support. There is a nurse manager who is in charge of all your Registered Nurses and LPN's. The nursing staff consists of nurses on duty 24 hours a day. They usually are also trained in hospice and palliative care. They are usually trained in pain management. There is a hospice medical director that supervises the medical care of the patient. A Psychologist are able to talk about facing a terminal illness and the end of life. The chaplain services give spiritual support during hospice. There is a social work staff that can help with finances and referrals to other agencies. The Pharmacist reviews all medicines and may suggest some to the doctor to control symptoms and comfort. The recreation therapist offers fun activities for both those in hospice and family members. One of them is Qigong which helps to promote physical, functional, social and emotional well being using an ancient Chinese system of movements, postures, breathing techniques, and meditations. The dietician helps the patient plan the best meals for his health. The housekeeping service keeps everything clean and orderly. Volunteers do services to help the family and patient with reading, playing games, and writing, or just visiting.

The hospice unit where he stayed offered day passes to go out, overnight passes, and week-long vacation stays if someone had a nice place to visit. Hospice does try to be flexible. What exactly is hospice, it is an end of life comfort that does not promote dying but rather accepts that death will come to all of us, and at this particular time it is made much more comfortable for the person who is going through the process. It is an act of grace from God the beautiful Creator who ultimately looks after us all.

Hospice Revealed

Hospice revealed, for it is not all black and white,
Some people are very ill and some have life to live,
DNR, do not resuscitate is not required, it's your
    decision,
It is for all patients, not just for cancer patients,
You may receive hospice for longer than six months,
You can choose the amount of care you need with your
    doctor,
Hospice care is a benefit of Medicare and Medicaid,
Questions call your local hospice center, God Bless...
SLB

If a loved one is in hospice, pray with all your heart for a miracle. Accept the decision God chooses, because that is ultimately God's plan. But our free will allows us to pray, hope, and ask God for a miracle. You ultimately want your loved one to find peace, whether that be through God, prayer or the gentleness you give to them. Peace is a treasure and the finest gift you can give to them.

There is power in the release of prayers:

1 Peter 5:7
Casting all your care upon him; for he careth for you.

2 Peter 3:9
The Lord is not slack concerning his promise, as some men count slackness; but is longsuffering to us-ward, not willing that any should perish, but that all should come to repentance.

Keep God First

Keep God first,
It was He who created you,
And to Him you shall go back,
Give Him your glory, your wisdom, your heart,
You shall be multiplied in blessings,
As the heavens to which shall you go,
Rejoice in the Lord,
Giving Him praise, Glory,
Abundantly, all you have...
SLB

There are many scriptures in the Bible that deal with healing. They are usually listed in the reference sections of Bibles. I am listing just a sample for you:

Psalm 147:3
He healeth the broken in heart, and bindeth up their wounds.

Revelation 22:2
In the midst of the street of it, and on either side of the river, was there the tree of life, which bare twelve manner of fruits, and yielded her fruit every month: and the leaves of the tree were for the healing of the nations.

Luke 8: 47-48
And when the woman saw that she was not hid, she came trembling, and falling down before him, she declared unto him before all the people for what cause she had touched him, and how she was healed immediately. And he said unto her, Daughter, be of good comfort: thy faith hath made thee whole; go in peace.

Jeremiah 3:22
Return, ye backsliding children, and I will heal your backslidings. Behold, we come unto thee; for thou art the Lord our God.

When you become more God-centered it is easier to ask for miracles and accept the small ones that do occur. How many times has something happened that you really thought twice about it. Something unexpected and you feel in your gut prayer must have influenced it, it could be a miracle. An excellent book very detailed and long is A Course on Miracles. You can check out www.miraclecenter.org/quotes for divine inspiration. This book will also give you inner strength. Becoming more God-centered is what usually happens when faced with a crisis or death situation. A very good goal would be to live in the now, to try to achieve the point where you feel you are God-centered, and to ask the Holy Spirit for guidance and wisdom. An excellent goal would be to be an act as Jesus would be. He is the only person without sin and truly we should aspire to that.

I Feel Closer Lord

I feel closer Lord,
While I sit in this social space,
This church,
    Your home,
Where I come for total peace,
Total clarity,
Total awe,
I hear your word,
I sing your praises,
Total adoration,
    To you on high,
I ask only to your ears,
    To hear my plea,
I plea for you to hear my heart,
To respond to my prayers,
    As only you can,
Because in this sanctuary,
I now call home,
I feel closer Lord,
Yes, closer to You...
SLB

Understand Life's Mysteries Of Trials

As the flames flicker,
I dare not want it now, Lord,
Can I change this outcome?
It is hard, so hard I cannot do it by myself,
And I reach out to You,
You alone have all answers,
You alone-Know,
The outcome I yet to know,
The trials and tribulations of my earthly life,
I ask yet of one concern,
Please God grant me Peace,
Grant me yet Peace,
Your Peace...
SLB

This is a list of seven steps that I put together to do at the beginning of each day. They can also be done any other time and this does not just have to be the patient. Please do this with the highest intention and with polite gratitude.

Step one-Deep Breathe-imagine yourself surrounded by a large bubble of protection. Now imagine angels surrounding you. The angels are holding you and showing you warmth and love. They are surrounding you with a large white healing light.

Step two-begin to bind all the negative energy that you have and give it to the angels to discard. After the negative has disappeared allow only the purest positive energy to flow within you, to enter your bubble.

Step three-Ask the Grace of God to flow directly through every cell in your body nourishing it with all the strength you will need.

Step four-Father in Jesus name, in the name of The Holy Spirit, "I need my miracle now." State your intention to God loud and clear, so that your ears also hear what you ask of the Lord.

Step five-Repeat out loud God is Love and Love is God while holding your hand on your heart, as many times as you feel necessary. Feel Jesus in your heart.

Step six-I am using cancer in my example, but please feel free to substitute any other illness or disease, thank you. Bind the cancer, and throw it out of my body, allow it to flow freely through and out my kidneys with no restrictions. I ask now at this time in my life to allow pure rejuvenated cells to flow through my body. I would ask for complete clarity in my mind. I want to balance my physical, spiritual, and emotional well being.

Step seven-Believe in this, "I will be completely healed, a man of God, in God's glorious vision, without complications, consequences, or conflict. I am. I am a Divine One. I am asking Jesus Christ of Nazareth to fill my body with the divine healing light and love. I am asking this in the holy name of Jesus the Son of God. I believe with all of my heart that Love will heal me.

Amen.

You become afraid of dying usually these feelings need to be worked on. Acceptance takes time, and that is why some people become very quiet because they become reflective on their lives and looking inside for the Divine within themselves. My gentleman once told me he was not afraid of leaving he was more worried about his quality of life while he was still alive. He said it was not about prolonging his life it was about the life he was living.

One passage with dying from the Bible is:

John 11: 25-26

Jesus said unto her, I am the resurrection, and the life, he that believeth in me, though he were dead, yet shall he live: And whosoever liveth and believeth in me shall never die. Believest thou this?

Sometimes during the process of hospice the person who is the caregiver finds it difficult, because they can't fix it. The care giver and the person in hospice each should love themselves. First love and accept yourself. Where there is self-love there is less self-abuse. No one is perfect in this world. Love yourself and do not reject yourself. Build your power from rest each day, love yourself and each will find an easier time through hospice.

Prayer is a constant during hospice. I went twice a day to the chapel exploring every prayer every bit of hope. It gives us great comfort. You can feel the closeness of God. He does understand. We need to understand we knew the outcome before we decided to come back into this life for our lesson. If we chose a hard lesson we will get stronger. Trust me I know difficulty. No one wants a bad outcome, we all hope for a miracle a cure. I did and if put in that situation again I can say I will again. I had five constant prayers and they were:

The Lord's Prayer

Our Father who art in heaven,
Hallowed be thy name,
Thy kingdom come,
Thy will be done,
On earth as it is in heaven,
Give us this day our daily bread,
And forgive us our trespasses,
As we forgive those,
Who trespass against us,
And lead us not into temptation,
But deliver us from evil,
For thine is the kingdom,
And the power,
Forever and ever,
Amen.

Powerful Prayer to The Holy Spirit

Holy Spirit,
    You who solve all problems; who light all roads, so that I can attain my goal. You who give me the Divine gift to forgive and to forget all evil against me and that in all instances of my life you are with me. I want this short prayer to thank you for all things and to confirm once again that I never want to be separated from you even in spite of all material illusions. I wish to be with you in eternal glory. Thank you for your Mercy toward me and mine.
    The person must say this prayer for 3 consecutive days, after 3 days the favor will be granted even if it may appear difficult. This prayer must be published immediately after the favor is granted without mentioning the favor. Only your initials should appear at the bottom. Thank you.

St. Jude's Novena

May the Sacred Heart of Jesus be adored, glorified, loved and preserved throughout the world, now and forever.

Sacred Heart of Jesus, pray for us, St. Jude, worker of miracles, pray for us.

Say this prayer 9 times a day and by the eighth day your prayer will be answered. It has never been known to fail. Thank-you St. Jude.

Prayer to The Virgin Mary

O Most Beautiful Flower of Mount Carmel, fruitful vine, Splendor of Heaven, Blessed Mother of the Son of God, Immaculate Virgin, assist me in this my necessity. O Star of The Sea, help me herein you are my Mother. O Holy Mary, Mother of God, Queen of Heaven and Earth, I humbly beseech thee from the bottom of my heart to succor me in my necessity (make request). There are none that can withstand your power. O show me herein you are my Mother. O Mary, conceived without sin, pray for us who have recourse to thee (3X). Holy Mary, I place this cause in your hand (3X). Thank you for your mercy to me and mine. Amen.

After three days publish this prayer with just your initials.

St. Theresa's Prayer

May today there be peace within. May you trust God that you are exactly where you are meant to be. May you not forget the infinite possibilities that are born of faith. May you use those gifts that you have received, and pass on the love that has been given to you. May you be content knowing you are a child of God. Let this presence settle into your bones, and allow your soul the freedom to sing, dance, praise, and love. It is there for each and every one of us. Amen.

One tends to be in constant prayer and that too is good. Without knowing you are drawing closer to God. God-who is first I your life, God-who sees your tears, feels your concerns and knows your every thought.

I Cannot Handle It Lord

I cannot handle it Lord,
    As I sit holding back my tears,
My tears of sorrow,
    Flow freely from my face,
Helplessly awaiting a word,
    A sign,
Yes Lord, I sit in your chapel,
A place of such peace,
Mine has been taken from me,
Crumbled, beneath my feet,
Yet, I come back,
Looking for hope,
    Can it be real?
I sit quietly,
I shiver,
Hoping you, draw near,
Candles they flicker, on the altar,
    I hold dear,
Quietly waiting for my lesson,
A word-so clear...
SLB

Initially in hospice you pray for the pain to stop. Relief will come, modern medicine with all its benefits will do wonders. Medicine is a gift, thank God. Will the pain return, yes it probably will, but doctors manage it by increasing the dosages and allowing life to be good. Life without pain or manageable pain is exactly what a person in hospice dreams of. Quality of life is essential, and when break through pain can also be managed life can be beautiful.

Always Remember To...

Always remember to...
Learn for each day brings forth new messages to
    understand,
Listen for in each message, there is something new to
    be shared,
Wonder for in that we expand our minds and seek new
    knowledge,
Share for to do that with someone we love, gives us
    back more than we gave them,
Play as if we were still a child, for innocence gives us
    peace, and play sometimes quiet,
Imagine for life gives us many opportunities, and we
    just imagine what we want,
Smile as if your lover just came through the doorway,
    and glanced at you,
Believe that all the signs you are given, is for a divine
    purpose yet to come,
Work for it truly brings us joy and happiness, as does
    play,
When we accomplish the work we began,
Whisper beautiful thoughts of seduction to your love,
To carry them off to sleep,
Cherish all that life has given you, whether good or bad
    and learn from it all,
Care about everyone, for we are all God's children,
Trust in that one true friend you carry in your heart,
Try to everyday wake up and be the best person you
    can be,
For that one special day in your life,
Pray to the Almighty Lord Our Savior for all our
    blessings,

Dream of a better world for our children and
     grandchildren,
Than we could ever imagine,
Wish for peace,
For in peace all mankind can lead a good and happy
     existence,
Sing for a song is a message to God of your joy,
That you live in His world,
Hope for with God all things are possible,
And one of God's gifts to us was hope,
Laugh for it is the medicine that cleanses your soul,
Purifies you and gives everyone around you joy,
Dance as if she carried you away,
And the song in her heart,
Melts you into her on the dance floor,
Love as the first time you saw her smile,
When you and her were truly one...
SLB

The person with the illness is the one walking the path. They are the only one walking that path. If you are the one that is their rock, remember that. All decisions after communication are ultimately theirs. They are walking the path with God. God will carry them when they cannot do it themselves. God knows our future and He is the only one that can change it. God puts people and places together as no other. We all come together for a reason, allow that circumstance to enrich your being.

Just As You Believed There Would Be A Sunset

Just as you believed there would be a sunset, to see,
    I truly, believe in good things for thee...
Believe, is a powerful word and thought God gave
    to man,
    With concentration and knowledge, "It" can...
So believe, have faith that God will provide,
    He gave you someone to help and be on your side...
Believe just as the first bird in spring will appear,
    God will give you the answer, ask, wait and hear...
Believe just as the Robins' left their nest,
    You will be healed in prayer as you rest...
Believe in the goodness that lies within all,
    And pray that they all shall hear God's call...
Believe that both of us have met our fate,
    You shall have the life you wish, with your mate...
Believe that all of our children will prosper and go far,
    For to us, each of them is a precious star...
Believe that Your Creator who lives in heaven above,
    Shall always fill your heart, with the utmost love...
SLB

Hospice allows the person growth. It is intended to teach and understand the dying process. Dying is not easy. It is not easy to leave this earth. We all are born and then die. It is what we do in between to help others and ourselves toward the betterment of humanity is what counts. We all cross to the other side some day. I also recommend reading books about dying and the process of dying. It is very helpful that you know that we are not alone in this world. There are people out there willing to help. The more you learn the better informed you will be during the process.

Death You See In Your Face Everyday

Death you see in your face every day,
  Most people don't understand, although
  some may...
Year after year complications arise,
  Asking again, dare he does need one more day to
  rise...
Understanding improbable, people don't want to hear
  your word,
  Silence you most keep, craving yet desperate, your
  voice to be heard...
My soul suffered not, what yours alas has,
  My soul suffered differently than yours has...
My soul sees death, yet in its own way,
  Praying to my Savior, to let my love stay...
Rendering sweet words of comfort and joy, to ease your
  pain,
  Never admitting my fears, for doing that, I might
  dare complain...
For death does look, yet to me, my sweet dear,
  It only allows me, my sweetheart to fear...
I must hold the memory of your beautiful face,
  And must carry on, and do it with grace...
For sorrow I must never, show to a soul,
  Every day contemplating onward, alas missing you
  whole...
Life seemed to you a struggle, as the years went along,
  Your sweetheart arrived, now-let her sing to you
  your song...
For we all must meet, our Savior, we love,
  Hold on to the symbol of our love, a dove...

I understand, I don't have, the answers you need,
Alas, once I did give you, Hope-a mustard seed...
Death will come-both to you and I, some sweet day,
I fear the loss of you, and for this I do pray...
For sweetheart, death I do not see in my face every day,
But death I must face in another, the most
sorrowful way...
My true love I have found him at last,
My heart still must go on-if his life alas is past...
So sweetheart please note, death it will come,
We will not know the day or night, it is from...
Your soul will be saved, and forever be free,
Always remember-smile down at me...
Come to me always, throughout each day,
Stay with me at night, while I pray...
Guide me to Heaven, meet me at the door,
For remember you always told me, you loved me
more...
SLB

Sunshine

You are the sunshine that brightens my every day,
Always giving me love, strength, and support
    your way...
May the Lord bless you and keep you, if it be God's will,
I will be there behind you, always precious ever still...
For it is your hand that always is there to hold,
I am your loving living angel I'm told...
We are as one in this conflict of fate,
Live life to its fullest, choose love not hate...
SLB

There can be days when you are feeling better and you just want to kick back and have a more normal day. It is days like that when going shopping, going out to lunch, going for a walk and just wanting simple pleasures to take over.

Take Me To A Place We Can Be Together

Take me to a place, we can be together,
    Running free and wild, as before,
    perhaps through the heather...
Take me to a place, where hurt doesn't exist,
    No health worries, no war, where I'm
    first on the list...
Take me to a place, where love's our only song,
    Where nothing I say, or do,
    Could ever be wrong...
Take me to a place, where hope is kind,
    Where everything I wish for, I need,
    Is not simply in my mind...
Take me to a place, perhaps the edge of space,
    Where love exists in everyone, no hatred,
    No worries, just one in God's race...
Take me to a place, where you and I can be one,
    That place does exist, I am God's daughter,
    And you are God's son...
SLB

Life in hospice becomes very appreciative. You awake and are grateful for one more day. One more day to praise the Lord and one more day for simple pleasures such as breakfast, sunshine, rain, stars, and the moon. Sundays you look forward to church and you hope you will never miss one. You start to enjoy the solo singers, the sermons, the going up toward the altar to pray, it gets in your blood. You wait for Wednesday mornings with homemade pancakes and if you can have a pass to go to the grocery store to buy blueberries to add them to the batter. Simple thoughts cross your head, which make you happy.

Appreciate life and be humble to the Lord who gave it to you. Every day you walk upon this Earth is a gift. When you are close to death you appreciate more. Whisper sweetly, I love you, to those closest to you, making their day as well as yours. Every breath you take allows you to give love and kindness back to those that mean so much to you. If you are given a second chance use it wisely.

Your life is your life and the only one God gave to you, so use it wisely. It is special and unique and oh so beautiful. Mine is filled with prayers and poetry, yours should be as unique as mine is to me. Whether we are here tomorrow or not use whatever time you have to the fullest. God gave us a little word and He called it Today. Today could be the most special day in your life so use it wisely. If you are a person who has faced Death, you are on God's time. Use it wisely.

Whether you are in hospice or not enjoy your life. Do what gives you pleasure whether going out to eat, the movies, for a walk, enjoy. Take good care of your body, emotions and spiritual life. Everyone talks about a bucket list but be realistic. Be thankful for living your life the best it can be. Remember there is a time for sorrow, a time for joy, and a time for everything in between. Bucket lists are seldom completed, but they give us a chance to dream. The chance to dream, the chance to see another sunrise or sunset is what is truly important.

See yourself with positive health. Don't dwell on the fact that you have this or that. Focus on what you do have. Focus on what makes you feel better. I recommend checking into enzymes, vitamins, herbs, water and perhaps a diet of 25% fresh raw fruits and vegetables. If you don't follow an exact routine have faith. Faith moves mountains. When you put positive thoughts into the universe you improve yourself. Project and imagine and it will happen.

Enjoy the moment. Life is good so live for the now. The present, absorb it, feel it and savor it with 100% of your being. Whether you are sick or have perfect health, do it now. Someone once told me if I am at my weakest, hooked up to tubes, what can I do? I want to be worthwhile for this world. I can pray. Pray for everyone you know. Pray for everyone that they know. Talk to God. He will listen. Pray and help others. By doing that you are helping yourself. We do not live alone. We are social beings. We interact with people on different levels. It is a wonderful thing when you realize how powerful your life can be through prayer. The simple yet effective, power of prayer. Pray for all that need help, in the simplest to the hardest of problems. You will feel it. You will feel a warmth in your heart, it is wonderful, hard to explain; but so beautiful only God could give that to you. Ask for others, and you shall receive for yourself.

Gratitude, be in constant gratitude toward God. Whatever He gives you, handle it. Accept it and Praise God and be grateful. He is allowing you the chance to help others. Be grateful your words can help and you can teach God's grace. God's blessings, you have that ability. Be grateful for the person He allows you to be, for He created you in the most perfect of images, His own. Be grateful He is your Creator, your God. I am grateful for every blessing God gives to me. My heart is filled with so much love toward God, it feels like it wants to burst open, and say: Believe, trust in God, thank you a million times over. When you feel it, it is like nothing else in the world, you fall upon your knees and you talk, really talk to God. You pour out your soul, even though He knows every cell of your body, and with as much gratitude as there are stars in the universe you praise Him, love Him, respect Him as no other could ever, or ever will be. Humble as you can, bow down to Him and offer unconditional love toward Him as he has given to you. You have gone inward to God, you truly are saved. You are one with God, and shall live with Him in eternal glory. Praise Him for His mercy upon your life and graciously accept Him, as "I am."

Let go of fear, for in letting go of fear you can replace it with the opposite which is love. Love is what is needed to get well. The purest love is that of God. Do not let fear be your life. Remember you have time. Don't rush, enjoy your time and fill yourself with joy.

If you ask the Lord for a miracle, be careful what you promise. He knows everything. If you promise write it down, keep yourself honest to God. Everyone asks in some way or manner, it is the absolute human thing to do. Accept your situation, if God gives you more time you have a miracle indeed. Thank Him and live your life as fully as you can. Be wise with your words and thoughts. Pray for everyone, pray for the angels that watch you, and for those that have gone before you. Pray for the saints and your masters that guide you. Never worry about yourself, others will do it for you. Love them and all shall be in its place.

Dear Lord of Mercy and Father of Comfort,

You are the one I turn to for help in moments of weakness and times of need. I ask you to be with your servant in his illness. Please send your healing word to your servant. In the name of Jesus, drive out all infirmity and sickness from his body. Dear Lord, I ask you to turn this weakness into strength, suffering into compassion, sorrow into joy, and pain into comfort for others. May your servant trust in your goodness, May your servant hope in your faithfulness, even in the middle

of this suffering. Let him be filled with patience and joy in your presence as he waits for your healing touch. Please restore your servant to full health. Dear Father, Remove all fear and doubt from his heart by the power of your Holy Spirit, and may you, Lord, be glorified through his life. As you heal and renew your servant, Lord, may he bless and praise you. All of this I pray in the name of Jesus Christ.
Amen.
SLB

I wrote some of these poems for those in hospice for comfort for both the patient and the care givers...

Every Day The Lord Has Given Us

Every day the Lord has given us,
I thank Him heart-fully,
To graciously allow us to be friends,
Has meant a lot to me...
The Lord has appeared before me,
And showed me His love,
He has allowed us to be together,
He has blessed us from above...
I say a couple prayers each day,
That you will win your fight,
It would mean so much to both of us,
If you would be alright,
You've suffered like other soldiers have,
From a war in a far off land,
Release all your inward pain,
That I might reach you and give you my hand...
Comfort-allow me to always give to you,
No more shall bad memories stay,
Beautiful thoughts embrace yourself,
From-henceforth this very day...
You have a passion set forth in me,
To bring you peace and joy,
For sweetheart, you alone shall always be my
    special boy...
SLB

Many Have Said There Are No Miracles Around

Many have said there are no miracles around,
　　Holidays can be magical, sit back, hear the sound...
Feel the fullness that a miracle may bring,
　　Your heart about to burst, your voice to sing...
It shall in all its' glory and might,
　　Your soul uplifted, doing everything right...
Bursting forth an understanding and healing that day,
　　Love blossomed ever further, so they say...
To a heavenly land where miracles flow,
　　Connections everlasting with the purest of a glow...
Happiness so beautiful, immeasurable out of sight,
　　It makes our souls soar, as cardinals in flight...
As we whispered together, a miracle occurred now,
　　Humbly kneeling together in prayer to worship
　　and bow...
Understanding of such, miracles do appear,
　　For those whom we love-and hold dear...
SLB

For I Lay My Head Upon Your Shoulder

For I lay my head upon your shoulder, as you lay,
Caressing you, oh so gentle, but firm so you know,
And I touch your hands, stroking them,
So your mind wanders, and never has pain,
And I draw my head to glance gently at your eyes,
And speak whispers of love that only you shall hear,
And my presence you feel, distances nonexistent,
We are as one, and together we pray,
As I cascade you back, into my world of emerald green,
    Rustic leaves, and endless skies,
As we glance upward, hand in hand, heat in heart,
We pray to Mother God, and Gracious Mother Mary,
To pour their golden hearts love,
Into that tube that feeds your medicine into you,
And my strength and my love as well,
Shall be poured, that only love,
Shall you feel, penetrated deeply into each cell,
Nourishing you and allowing the medicine,
That Our Lord enabled healers to help you,
And give you strength, to work for health, to heal,
And I lay cuddling my legs into yours,
You feel me totally, as I am with you,
Taking all that I can, and leaving you with only love,
For I have poured into you, my love,
As you did to me, so many times...
SLB

I Want To Hold You All Over To Ease Our Pain

I want to hold you all over, to ease the pain,
To erase from your memories, all sickness and sorrow,
Let me bare it for you, at least until tomorrow,
Come close as I touch, and unstill your fate,
Tiny touches of love, shall pacify your heart,
If not for gotten, renounced for a while,

I want to hold you all over, to ease your pain,
Let me take it upon me, come close as I whisper,
Release all your hurt, suppressed through it may be,
Let only pure energy flow in thee,
Surround your heart with mine,
Let me hold the burden you bare,
Though it may be not forever,
At least while we share...
SLB

Never Forget Who Created The Flowers

Never forget who created the flowers,
  Never forget who put the inspiration into the man,
  Who created the towers...
Never forget to kneel down and pray,
  Never forget who created the suns' ray...
Never forget God did give you a tough row to hoe,
  Never forget God at birth, gave you ten fingers and
  ten toe...
Never forget you are not in this alone,
  Never forget he told Edison to invent the phone...
Never forget you have someone, that does care,
  Never forget God gave you me, to be able to share...
SLB

What Is Cancer?

This is re-written from the original version in my own
   words...

What cancer cannot do?
Cancer is so limited,
It cannot cripple love,
   Love will grow stronger, if you believe in God
   above...
It cannot shatter hope,
   Hope will carry us through, and God will help us
   cope...
It cannot corrode faith dear,
   Faith increases, when your heart surrounded by
   God is near...
It cannot destroy peace, be still,
   Let peace surround you, it is God's will...
It cannot kill friendship,
   Friendship grows to love, with one kiss on my lip...
It cannot suppress memories so sweet,
   New memories will be made, what a treat...
It cannot silence courage, hon,
   You've shown courage, you've won...
It cannot invade the soul,
   Soul turns to God, and now is completely whole...
It cannot steal eternal life,
   Life in the future, filled with no strife...
It cannot conquer the spirit,
   Spirit will shine, with God the light is lit...

This is a lovely tribute to those afflicted with cancer. It is a positive mental attitude walk. It is located at Florida Community College in Jacksonville, Florida. There are fourteen statements there listing how to conquer cancer.

Cancer Survivor Park

Strolling through the Richard and Annette Bloch,
   Cancer Survivor Park,

I felt peace and hope for survivors who had come here
   to leave their mark...
A small stream rolled over pebbles and stones,
   In the background, I heard chirping birds releasing
   hopeful tones...
Five bridges of beige, red, yellow, blue, and green,
   I would walk upon to pray the cancer is clean...
A sculpture, out front states cancer...'There's Hope,"
   Fourteen plagues providing words to help cope...
I prayed on the positive mental attitude walk,
   Contemplating serious thoughts, I did not talk...
Your fight is still not over my dear,
   Trust in the Lord, your doctors, and don't allow
   fear...
Advanced cures will fight this disease every day,
   We will return to this par, when you are cured and
   pray...
Thank you dear Lord for all you have done,
   This battle soon shall be over, "He has won"...
SLB

These poems are written for comfort...

May Your Chemotherapy Be Easy To Bare,

May your chemotherapy be easy to bare,
Just a few more times, your burden, I do care ...
May it be over sooner than we think,
Just let the pain disappear, quicker than a blink...
God will guide you through, providing calm, you
    belong,
I will pray each day, as miracles flow along...
For two to share chemo, will be easier to go through,
    today,
Count on me to be there, even if I'm far away...
SLB

May I Always Look Upon Your Face

May I always look upon your face,
    And see my man full of courage and grace...
May I always feel, such loving and care,
    And treat you with heartfelt respect, and always
    fair...
May you always look across the room, and turn me on,
    And with loving whispers, say my name as hon...
Yes, please my love always be my number one,
    Love me, keep me company, but always be fun...
SLB

When I talked to my gentleman about his main concerns during hospice, he stated five main concerns.

1) Spiritual health-a strong relationship with God
2) Relationship with your partner
3) Relationship with family
4) Health-God is the healer. Be proactive in your health.
5) Relationship with church family and friends

He said, "Have a strong faith in God, because God is in control. Our Shepherd, He has all the power."

Spiritual Connections through Meta-space...

You Asked To Be Healed

You asked to be healed,
God please hear this plea,
I love him so much,
He means everything to me,
Let us pray,
It is God's will,
Let no harm come to you,
From your treatments, I pray...
SLB

It is a good idea to have these papers in order when you are in hospice. I also have a set of these papers for myself. The first is an advance directive for a natural death ('Living Will"). This document should be given to your health care providers. They are instructions to withhold or withdraw life-prolonging measures in certain situations. There is no legal requirement for anyone to execute a living will. You should also name a person as your health care agent. You need to be comfortable giving that person broad and sweeping powers to make health care decisions for you. There is no legal requirement that anyone execute a health care power of attorney.

There are many good websites, pamphlets and other literature describing hospice and palliative care. Some may give you questions to consider at the end of life, some may explain options to you. I wrote this book in another manner explaining from a personal view, one who lived in a hospice environment for six months, and he got out of the hospice hospital and lived nine more months. I have used my thoughts as well as poetry to reinforce my feelings. Although this may be a less than conventional way of talking about hospice I do help it helps. Thank you

A Beacon Of Hope

A beacon of hope, given to thee,
When entering hospice, keep hope open,
Life can change, as fast as a river changes course,
Miracles do happen, that is what we call belief,
Keep your heart open for such a gift,
Accept what God gives to you,
Wish everyone tens of blessings,
Always be open to:
A beacon of hope, given to thee...
SLB

Hope

Hope is what we have been given,
Embrace it,
For through love and truth,
We will flourish and win,
We will win, for through all things with God are
    possible,
God is Love...
SLB

I AM

I AM Divine One
It will go away
Ask Jesus for divine healing of light and love,
Love will heal you...

Know God is in charge,
Let it Be...

Chapter 3
Ideas To Help Through Hospice

A person I respect told me this wise piece of advice,
"All you can do is plant a seed, an idea"...

1) Music
2) Nature
3) Arts and Crafts
4) Food
5) Simple Pleasures
6) Animals
7) Games and Movies
8) Friends
9) Total Love

I will be healthy
I will be alive
I will be healthy from health ailments
I will always be there for you
We will have a wonderful life in the future

Music...

This is a beautiful message from Martin Luther

"Next to the Word of God music deserves the highest praise. The gift of language combined with the gift of song was given to man that he should proclaim the Word of God through music."

Music is to me as others a very pleasant constant in my life. It does sooth the soul and provides calm for the body. It is extremely important and should be used for therapy and relaxation in hospice. It raises the vibration of the world and you are able to cope more with situations.

I was told classical music heals. There is beauty in Bach, Beethoven and Strauss. I believe that music is healing in the form that helps the person concerned. Every soul has a note, its perfect pitch. Just as we sing the note Hue to honor God before going into meditation. Music gives you a rush of energy while tuning your inside vibrations. It rejuvenates you as well as uplifting your creativity. Music will vibrate your internal organs and energize them.

I felt tears in my eyes when a group of singers would come into the hospice center and sing good old fashioned gospel music. You could feel the pull of the music being sent to the patient as well as up to heaven. It was so beautiful. There was a church service for the patients were we sang many gospel songs and lead by a simple piano. It was inspiring to those that attended. My favorite was when we sang How Great Thou Art. It is a beautiful hymn that lifts our hearts up to God. We also went to as many musical events that we could. We knew that music is uplifting, and whatever kind of music they offered us we appreciated it all. In many hospice centers there are concerts, pianos, and various types of music options available to listen to. I would encourage anyone to make full use of them.

There are many songs that we listened to and I even sang to him in hospice, one of them that I thought was very appropriate was by Garth Brooks "If Tomorrow Never Comes." It makes you want to appreciate all you have today. Let tomorrow handle itself and live for today.

I Want To Sing New Songs To You

I want to sing new songs to you,
　　To help you reach new heights of joy anew...
Sing to the Lord above today,
　　As this will take my cares away...
For song fills our hearts with love,
　　Just like we received a sign of the dove...
Music I'll teach you, you must surely learn,
　　I sang my life long, it is now your turn...
Sweet music will fill our night, so long,
　　And refresh our hearts, and make them strong...
This is God's will, that music be a part of your life,
　　It will bring you joy, and take away your strife...
So listen each day, and fill your heart with song,
　　Your sweetheart, will help you as you go along...
So will constantly love you, oh so much,
　　And through her love, you will feel her touch...
So listen while she sings sweet songs for you,
　　This is a special message from God, its true...
SLB

I Want to Sing Praise Songs to You

I want to sing new songs to you.

Remember Your Favorite Songs

Remember your favorite songs,
Yesterday comes to mind, an old Beatles hit,
Music should surround your heart,
For it makes your soul happy,
Dance in your chair if it be your will,
It gives harmony and joy to your life,
The best therapy's are often those we hear each day,
The melodies of a good song,
And those who wish to dance along...
SLB

Your Battle Is Not Quite Over

Your battle is not quite over,
But you are putting up quite a fight,
We ask the Lord to help you,
Fight this battle each and every day,
With complications, may they be gone,
And happiness fill your tears,
Difficulties please subside,
Let only goodness filter in,
No one of us should go this path alone,
Of this, you should be completely sure,
Let love surround your every turn,
And laughter fill the air, let music be sung,
From up on high,
As our miracle, please-shall it appear...
SLB

I <u>Will</u> Sing And Make Music With All My Soul,

I will sing and make music with all my soul,
  Together, serving our Lord, every day, making us
  complete and whole...
Give thanks to the Lord, for He is good; His love
  endures forever,
  Together, trusting in one true Holy Lord, to forget
  this never...
He has made everything, beautiful in its time,
  Together, truth shall be with us, as church bells do
  chime...
I will sing of the love of the Lord forever,
  Together, building a Christian life, our love will
  endeavor...
Live in peace and the God of love and peace will be
  with you,
  Together, happily ever after us we both say I do...
If we love each other, God lives in us,
  Together, teaching and helping every one love God,
  and thus...
SLB

You Sang Me A Song

You sang me a song, you are my sunshine,
    Making me appreciate the fact you are mine...
You studied and learned how to cook,
    So proud, I will give you a copy of my book...
Shepherd's pie you were so proud to make,
    Later that week, brownies you did bake...
You see eventually a baker you will be,
    You will be picking your pie apples from a tree...
SLB

Dancing, Dancing

Dancing, dancing, dancing is all you do, since you
    learned to tango,
        I thought you went way down to Mexico, to buy a
        mango...
Go get them tiger! Show them how you can disco,
        Thought you would make dinner, but you couldn't
        find the Crisco...
Now, you can dance and you are the star of the show,
        Hey wait a minute, first you need to do the lawn,
        go mow...
You are the king of the jungle since you can dance,
        Mesmerizing the senoritas into a trance...
I see you are swinging, you have rhythm, you are not
    meek,
        Better play hide and seek, when I get there you're
        up a creek...
SLB

Nature...

The best advice for both the caregiver and the patient is to totally enjoy each moment God gives to you. It doesn't have to be fancy, but in your mind give it quality. Many options and opportunities will be given to you, try to take advantage of them, for in doing so you are ultimately giving both of you a better life during this process. This does not mean you give up, it means having a quality existence.

This is what I did, I used all the best I had and I did not save things for a rainy day. I gave the best, because when you are faced with that news your thought processes change. I gave him facials, with ten steps and probably better than most women get at salons; reflexology with the finest oils, scented creams and best techniques, and different types of massage and body treatments whether therapeutic or relaxation. We listened to beautiful music and I sang, yes the best I could loud and clear and with meaning, in which every word came to life. We watched movies at the theater or first run movies in the room. They had become available to us in hospice. So we laughed at the funny movies and cried at the sad ones. We watched in suspense the guy flicks and enjoyed the girl flicks. We took long walks even if I was pushing a wheelchair or later when he had an electric scooter. Nature is fabulous for therapy.

One time when I was at my lowest during the endless days and nights of hospice, I walked outside, unaware the sunshine would come upon my face. It enriched me and it filled me with the peace from God. I took him for a walk and we both understood the power of nature. God is giving us peace; that comes from the sun upon your head or the warmth of the day.

Nature helped us. We saw the beauty God gives us through the trees, the flowers, and the animals. The colors and the elements in nature give off energy through the vibrations they give off. Nature brings us harmony and walking nourishes your soul. Our souls came alive again, for you see the type of diagnosis is harsh, and you need God, and His nature nourishes us into an appreciation just enough to forget our troubles while seeing the majesty of God's glory. You feel refreshed gazing upon the lake, the geese, and the cute little baby geese. The beautiful gardens and walkways healed both of us as we felt God within us at all times.

Savor the beauty of each sunny day, listen to the sounds of the quiet rain against the window, make sure to take time to see as many sunsets as you can imagine, and remember to walk outside in the quiet of the night and look up toward the stars in amazement. When you see a rainbow you are being blessed twice. God might say, "I'm here and I'm listening from nature." Every season and every day brings us new enjoyments that God has given us through nature.

Earthing is a concept of grounding oneself on Mother Earth for healing. Your feet should be planted on Earth, sand, or something made from Earth, as wood, ceramic tile, and they should remain there for about a half hour each day for maximum benefit. It is becoming more widespread as the simple idea is spreading. Earthing improves the auto-immune system. The body has the capacity to heal itself. Walking barefoot and grounding yourself to the Earth is very healthy. I especially love the sand, walking barefoot by the ocean. It also helps inflammation, fibromyalgia, improves sleep, chronic pain, arthritis, energy, lowers stress, adds calmness in your body, helps with your blood pressure, jetlag, and speeds healing. Earthing is power healing. Earthing restores you, we need to get back to walking on our earth and not cement.

Living One Day At A Time

Living one day at a time,
Enjoying one moment at a time,
Accepting hardships,
As the pathway to peace,
Taking as He did, this sinful world as it is,
Not as I would have it,
Trusting that He will make all things right,
If I surrender to His Will,
That I may be reasonably happy in this life,
And supremely happy with Him,
Forever, in the next.
SLB

Glide Away To Our Special Spot

If you are in pain this week, my dear,
Glide away to our special spot that is near...
A piece of the park, so close by the bay,
Escape there, even in your mind, night or day...
Soak the rays of the sun inside,
Listening to the ocean waves glide...
Smell the scent of that magical day,
Holding me close, everything else, fading away...
Dreaming beautiful thoughts inside,
As we picnic leaving troubles aside...
I'll sing to you songs listen to its beat,
Soon you will be dancing and moving those feet...
Be happy this day and ever other along,
These tiny thoughts helping sorrow and wrong...
SLB

Endearing You Are

Endearing you are, such words spoken by you,
  Love such as this, never experienced, so true...
Heartfelt expressions and sentiments you give,
  Expressing wishes and prayers for us to live...
Devotion I have learned, as I would give to you,
  Messages of hope, new avenues, such as Hue...
We have definitely grown over this year,
  Endearing you are, never letting me shed one tear...
We have shared and learned, even going to the park,
  It is a gift from heaven, to see its beauty and hear a
  lark...
So thank you my love, for saying how endearing I am,
  I feel exactly the same for you, my angel lamb...
SLB

Let's Go For A Walk

Let's go for a walk, along autumns' way,
   We will walk together, at the dusk of day...
Trample along with our feet through the leaves,
   Then turning together and feeling a cool breeze...
Hinckley Lake we'll go for a boat ride or two,
   Connecting us next time to sail away, me and you...
Let's rustle and listen to the leaves, orange and gold,
   Strolling I'll serenade to you, singing pretty I was
   told...
SLB

We Have A Special Place On Tampa Bay

We have a special place on Tampa Bay to pray,
    Where we talk to Jesus any time of day...
It is here He heard our message of great concern and
    care,
    As we said our prayer of healing, that he alone can
    spare..
This place it seems like heaven, for just the two of us,
    The water so pretty below our feet, we do not cuss...
I see St. Pete and Tampa by the shoreline, so fair,
    The manatees and sailboats serene, as they share...
Catch a bit of sunshine as the cool wind bustles in,
    A quiet place to sit alone, or bring your next of kin...
We thank the Lord for all good things,
    Especially this special place as we fly away on angel
    wings...
SLB

The Love Of This Land

The love of this land, so bare yet rich,
    Looking to the right, I see a revolutionary ditch...
It gives my love reason, that winter has come,
    Seeing it through his eyes I do, alas just some...
My eyes can now focus, absorb they will,
    North Carolina is clear, this land of Bill...
Tree limbs have lost all color, so soon,
    Yet skies lighten up through our Galactic moon...
Brooks and creeks appear now in sight,
    Covered by woods, they are their height...
The land that was his, the earth now clear,
    God gave us these seasons, to appreciate my dear...
SLB

So Let's Enjoy Each Sunset

Strolling along Simmons Park by the bay,
    Remembering a sacred message from Christ, on
    that special day...
I slowly glide my feet in the sand,
    Feeling mother natures' pull and force of this
    spiritual land...
A small white bird comes to me with her smile,
    Welcoming me back after my walk of almost a
    mile...
Splashing along humming a God sent tune,
    I wish I could have witnessed all of God's
    magnificence since noon...
But I came to see the sunset, and describe it to
    my man,
    Orange behind a cloud of mist, a beautiful
    symbolic fan...
St. Pete is peeking out so distant, yet so near,
    A bird comes to bring me a message, and drops one
    single tear...
The daisy that I picked, has surely washed to sea,
    I found the message inside of it, he really loves me...
A glance to find the perfect, yet impossible to find,
    A perfect little seashell, to captivate his mind...
So many little treasures can be found by the bay,
    Perhaps it was Christ's portrait, I shall remember
    on that day...
We asked our Lord for mercy and to give you health
    and joy,
    I'll never ask for a more perfect gift, than that for
    my beautiful boy...
So let's enjoy each sunset, as many as we can,
    Our favorite beach is calling us, me and my
    beautiful man...
SLB

My Connection With Nature And
Humanity Comes From Your Heavenly Grace

I walked down to the waters' edge, at the bay,
   Blue pastel colored skies and hues of pink, told that
   time of day...
When lovers come to stroll, and I but dream of you,
   My toes tingle in the water, so clear and blue...
Tonight the calm set in, a wave was not seen,
   I looked out, but not one wave, did lean...
And the ripples in the water so quiet they lay,
   Reflecting above from the sand from earlier
   that day...
A beautiful bird flew in the sky to draw my attention
   dear,
   Serene and quiet this paradise, not even a wave
   would I hear...
Looking up to heaven, I saw the sky, with quiet shades
   of gray,
   Peaceful thoughts surrounded me, as I began to
   pray...
Such magnificence you've given us, in this serene place,
   My connection with nature and humanity comes
   from your heavenly grace...
Thank you Lord for allowing me to see your beauty there,
   The ocean's so dear to me, I know I'll always care...
SLB

The Wonder Of This Golf Course

The wonder of this golf course, I truly feel,
 Ravishing its hues of emerald green, so real...
Contemplating ideas while in the midst of play,
 Planning magical journeys, right here, today...
For time stands still in the uniqueness of this quiet
 game,
 Thoughts of silence, contemplations, never the
 same...
As I play, the wind gathers its wishes to me,
 As I am to the wind, forever I'm free...
As the bird does walk along the side of the lake,
 I think pleasant dreamy thoughts, for my names
 sake...
For sometimes I sit, as I wait here to swing,
 Deep thoughts of devotion, to God shall I sing...
Peace, love and nature are all found out here,
 Golf is yes a game, but more meaning can be drawn,
 dear...
If you open your mind up, and allow it to wander,
 You might reach the next pinnacle of development,
 way up yonder...
So listen to the wind, along the way,
 Enjoy golf, and worship nature and God all through
 the day...
SLB

That's My World

Turn and suddenly see another miracle of His creation,
  Beauty is with us all, even in my part of this
  nation...
Great blue herons cross my street, and my backyard
  walk,
  Listening to a ruddy duck, in Grantham park...
Putting my feet in the water, pinfish, gray snapper, and
  tarpon appear,
  A diamondback terrapin turtle lives on my golf
  course, dear...
Running to the shore, I see West Indian Manatee,
  Sitting on my porch, a deer I see...
Welcome to my world, the space so green,
  Saw Palmetto, turtle grass, and Florida royal palm,
  I have seen,
My piece of heaven, when I ride my cart,
  Pumping energy through my soul, my heart to
  start...
Yes moon jelly fish, sea nettle, and also a cushion sea
  star,
  And then gaze at the universe, oh so far...
God out did himself, when he created my space,
  I look at Simmons beach and see His face...
Turn and see another, perhaps a ghost crab,
  Enjoy all this beauty, it is truly fab...
SLB

Arts and Crafts, Colors...

Life in hospice allows many patients the opportunities to try new and exciting things. Occupational therapy teaches projects such as leather working, ceramics, painting, ornament making, woodwork projects, and more. It's a golden opportunity to enjoy and meet new friends.

Green is the healing color and color is a very important tool of healing. Modern medicine is acknowledging alternative medicine as having many different aspects to healing and respecting them. Edgar Cayce over seventy years ago talked about the benefits of color when used in healing. I would check out colors for healing various problems you may have because in all honesty it is a detailed study.

A fun idea is to make a poster and on the top say Gratitude. On it list all the things you are grateful for. Make sure to say thank you for all that you have. I put that poster in a place I could take out and show him when he needed a little encouragement. It stated to be grateful for your life, no matter what God has given to you, it is your life. Schedule your time and use it wisely. Keep a list of what you would like to get done, such as attend a movie next week, go to pottery class, finish a puzzle. Whatever it is it is important for you. Remember God put us here to enjoy ourselves, so have fun with whatever you are doing at the time.

I love to take pictures recording my life in snapshots. In today's age they would call them "selfies". It is important for you to take pictures, videos, tape record recordings for yourself and your family. They are cherished memories to keep forever. Working on photos books enables you to reminisce about where you were when you took the photos and what you want to tell others about your experience.

I know some ladies that can get more things done than you can imagine. They are multitasking and making lovely crocheted, knitted, or embroidered items while also watching television or visiting. At hospice centers they encourage people to take up these crafts. The occupational therapists are trained in this to help and encourage you. Homemade lap blankets are also welcomed by those in wheelchairs needing warmth and the love crocheted into them. I still have the one given to us by my cousin Terry, and made with love.

That special time of year encourages us to make Christmas decorations and ornaments, to give as gifts and use ourselves. It is uplifting when you create with your own hands. The gathering of people all working on various projects, giving each other ideas and inspiration can bring much joy. I worked on Christmas projects I had ideas from my childhood, and gave them away to the nurses. The staff becomes a family unit to you and the love in your heart wants to give. That is natural and so beautiful to feel for other humans that are in care positions toward you.

The making of pottery or the painting of your ceramics can be very therapeutic. The whole process from picking out what you are going to do, molding the clay, having it fired and then working on painting it is exciting. It is the mingling of friends being proud of what they are making and showing others, and when you are a part of it you feel the genuine warmth. We were put here to make beautiful objects and to enjoy them. All that we do goes back to honoring Our Creator.

Puzzles can turn into framed artwork as I have seen at the hospice center. These are 1000 piece puzzles or larger that several people work on together, with great pride. You can work on an individual puzzle and it helps keep your mind very active. It's simple but very rewarding. We worked on several and he was so proud when they were hung up with his name on them.

On Magic Wings May You Fly

On magic wings may you fly,
  Soaring up unto the sky...
Fulfilling your dreams of people yet to meet,
  Helping your Lord in good deeds I think...
Give all you have to projects my dear,
  Your reward will be twice back next year...
Your heart has a gift of love so true,
  It has to be shared with others by you...
The Lord above is thanking you through me,
  So go to what drives you, for you will see...
The Lord will always bless and watch over you,
  This calling from Our Lord enriches you too...
SLB

135

Food and Special Treats...

The most beautiful and gracious act you can do before eating your food is to bless it. It is a ritual that has been passed down through the generations. When you bless your food by thanking the Lord for what you are to partake of you are promoting better nutrition and healing. It is thought that the vibrational levels of food are raised by the blessing. It is also a good idea to bless the preparation of the food and that the food we eat is giving our bodies exactly what it needs for its well being. This is especially important for those with ill health. When you pray ask that the food that you eat nourishes the correct parts of your body that need it at that time. You may also do that for supplements and vitamins, herbs, oils, and anything pertaining to the betterment of our bodies.

The importance of a proper diet and the importance of balancing what you eat should be considered. I am a Certified Nutritional Consultant (CNC). Anyone who has studied nutrition can put you on a proper diet. I have found in reality do the very best you can for what is causing your body not to be in balance, and if you want to splurge and enjoy yourself go ahead, sometimes that is what we need for the spirit.

The basics of health are simple and they include a good diet, exercise, and a good mental and spiritual attitude. This becomes complicated in everyone due to everyday living, stress, and complications we did not ask for. Keep the attitude that you will try and improve yourself, even if it is a little at a time.

One of the ideal goals in a diet would be 75% healthy Alkaline and 25% Regular Acid. Examples of this are meat, poultry and fish are very acidic. Dairy products are acid, cereals and grains are acid and fresh fruits and vegetables are alkaline. There is a lot to consider when food planning and much has gone into how to ideally combine various foods. Try to include protein but not in excess portions, remembering vegetables more on the plate. Also remember to watch your salt, coffee, tea, soda drinks, and snack foods daily so they are not in large quantities. For every individual case I would consult a professional for everyone is different, so please use this as a stepping stone to ask a professional dietitian further questions.

Another important idea when you are developing a diet, if you can eat your food and especially your fruits and vegetables 80% raw and 20% cooked. When incorporating this idea food will be as a medicine, and not just as enjoyment. You should try to eat local foods from farmers as much as possible. This is food grown within a fifty mile radius of your home. The food in this region is in a natural rhythm to your body. When traveling try the local food, when doing this it helps your body to adjust to the area. When you are food combining, try moderation and balance. Try to eat well at home so you can go a little crazy when you go out. Get out there and enjoy all you can. When your appetite comes back, enjoy. Don't worry about a thing. Take this as an opportunity to try those restaurants you always wanted. Hospice usually allows patients to leave and enjoy culinary treats around the city and with your doctors' permission sometimes a special treat of wine or beer. Deserts, coffee houses, ice-cream stands just have fun, food also is good for your soul, so enjoy.

Do not forget the importance of water on healing. Eight to ten glasses of fresh pure water not substitutes, just water. It flushes your body of impurities and keeps your body as healthy as it can be. Water a true gift from God. There are many ideas on what is the best water to drink for your body. I feel as long as you drink purified drinking water and 8-10 glasses a day you are keeping your body working the way it was intended to work.

Herbs and herbal remedies are something to be considered in hospice. The use of herbs dates back to before Biblical times. Herbs are used in medicines throughout the world. Some modern medicines are inspired by old fashioned herbal remedies. Herbs have become popular again in the last twenty years. Herbs are sometimes used alongside modern prescription drugs. Herbal remedies are a gift from Mother Earth. Consult a professional when deciding on which herbs to incorporate into your health regime.

Supplements such as certain juice blends as Jusuru life blend may be advised. Consult a professional. I have used a juice blend which gives you healthier joints, better skin, and healthy aging. The one that I use is Jusuru has a formulation which provides Biocell collagen II, Resveratrol, and Antioxidants from twelve super fruits. There are many juice blends and they do help lead a healthier life.

Vitamins and Minerals can be beneficial to those in hospice. Depending on the particular person you would be wise to consult a professional concerning what would help you. I would advise to take less. Take about three to five different vitamins or minerals and then change what you are taking ever so many months to give your body a chance to use them where they are needed. A good all purpose vitamin is always, Vitamin C as well as what your particular body needs.

Fasting is recommended to help with any illness, because through fasting the body can rest and recover. Sometimes fasting to some people is considered a spiritual experience. During fasting the body does not have to concentrate on digesting food. And it can rid the body of the toxins that might be causing an illness. Fasting when done regularly helps the organs rest, especially the liver, kidneys and colon. There are definite times and ways to fast. Sometimes with certain conditions you may become worse before better and that is due to the rapid elimination of toxins overloading the kidneys, lungs, liver and skin. After fasting certain foods have to be started in certain ways. It is always a good idea to read up on fasting, and become familiar. Please remember fasting should always be discussed with your personal physician, because they can discuss the overall benefits and help you decide how long a fast, and if perhaps, short repeated fasts versus one long fast would be more beneficial.

I Know How To Get To A Man's Heart

I know how to get to a man's heart, through his
    tummy,
    Delicious breakfasts, lunches, and dinners that he
    calls yummy...
I bought you delicious ice-cream,
    Wow, you ate so much, I caused you to scream...
I make a mean cup of coffee,
    If you're good, you also get a little toffee...
With Beckerovka, I've showed you the best,
    Turkey and a piece of pie, put you down to rest...
I take some eggs and make them a scramble,
    Potatoes, toast, and bacon and it's a ramble...
Who makes the best picnics to eat by the sea,
    Answer that wisely, it better be me...
Yes, I know the way to a man's heart,
    Start working in the kitchen right from the start...
Remember, this gal is a great cook,
    She might surprise you and even write a book...
SLB

Surprise Me With A Gift

Surprise me with a gift, you did make,
 You spent some time in the kitchen, and did bake...
Five delicious brownies or an ice-cream cone,
 Wanting to pick up my cell and phone...
But I had an afternoon treat,
 So delicious it nearly knocked me off my feet...
The absolute best brownie, I ever did eat,
 Don't ever send those goodies to the southern
 heat...
I will save one for Monday thru Friday,
 Let's celebrate learning to bake, a special way...
Always remember that gesture, it was so kind,
 Going off my diet, and I really didn't mind...
Because I know the love you baked into those five,
 That's so much fun, making us come and feel alive...
SLB

Simple Pleasures...

The pleasure of just being...
Treat yourself well...
Visualize it and it will be yours...visualize that you are free
of pain and a healthy person. Relax and see the pictures in your
head of your future. Use your imagination to see this happen.

Simple pleasures are the greatest to fill up your days.
Walking through the corridors of the hospice unit and finding
a Starbucks for a decaf Cinnamon Latee coffee. Bingo games,
secretly hoping it would be the night for either a free donut or
better yet a hotdog. Winning money at bingo the big two dollar
prize suddenly became the news of the week. When you are in
this position, God gives you an important lesson. You feel what
others feel. No matter how you feel, no matter how impossible
your situation may seem, others may be worse off. You gain
new compassion. You gain growth. You gain sensitivity to put
others needs ahead of yours, and you know, God is good, God is
great.

Always keep your Lord God above everyone else. Thank Him
for all He Has given to you. Be always grateful. Ask the universe
for what will make you happy. Give everything its due time. Be
patient. Have faith in all who love you. Know your significant
other is not going any place, but is solid. She loves the Lord,
and understands the full meaning and that everything has a
purpose. Our karma needs to be completed. Keep in constant
communication with Jesus, God, and the Holy Spirit, the Saints,
and your angels. Help at least one person a day and wish a
stranger on the street for God to protect and guide them as
well. When you give out love you get love in return.

Another simple pleasure and very simple is the art of
breathing. Just below your naval take in deep breathes in and
out holding them for 15 seconds if possible. Think of yourself at
the same time as clearing your aura. This also helps to center
oneself. Deep breathing and taking in oxygen is very healthy.

Another ritual is going outside when the stars and moon are at their loveliest and asking the Divine as you deep breath in and slowly excel your air to bless you as you thank him for the air He give our bodies to breathe and the life force it is. Ask for the life force of fresh oxygen to penetrate your body as you say your gratitude to God for providing it to you.

Reflexology-I am a Certified Reflexologist from the Institute of Reflexology in St. Petersburg, Florida. I strongly believe in the healing touch that we give. While my gentleman was in hospice I gave him up to four sessions a day of reflexology. When he experienced a new setback or new health issue I would immediately address that issue. I asked the Divine to take over my hands in the most beneficial for him, allowing the healing energies to pour forth.

Aromatherapy is one of the many forms of alternative medicine. King Solomon believed in the incredible healing of oils. The keeper of the oils was quiet, for it was he, who knew the secret of the vibration of oils. Aromatherapy uses volatile plant materials known as essential oils, the pure essence of a plant. The intention is for physical healing and the balancing of emotions. Essential oils have the ability to pass through the epidermal barrier, because they are oil soluble not water soluble. They enter the bloodstream and are considered safe and nontoxic. There are four different types of applications: direct inhalation, aerial diffusion, topical applications, and spiritual applications. The spiritual applications have been documented in both the New and Old Testaments in the Bible. Please remember this safety information. The oils are very powerful and there are safety guides to be taken. This is especially important if you are considering using them in hospice. There are benefits to the use of essential oils such as they fight harmful microbes, they balance bodily functions, they raise bodily frequencies, they are used as antioxidants that will purify our systems, they help emotional issues that are negative, and they are used in spiritual work. Use 100% pure essential oils because synthetic scents can have negative effects and side effects. Always consult a professionally trained person who fully understands aromatherapy.

I am a Certified Natural Health Practitioner (CNHP) and as such am able to make Bach flower formulas to aid our total health. Bach flowers are used to provide remedies of physical and psychological dilemmas. It is based on the theory that all of the flowers used have different emotions. Nature is a healer as God intended it to be. Bach flower remedies work on several moods which are identified in those that are sick; and they are fear, terror, worry, indecision, uncertainty, indifference, apathy, doubt, discouragement, over caring, weakness, impatience, self-distrust, over enthusiasm, pride or aloofness. A simple formula is made up following a series of questions and the decision on what to concentrate on for the best interest of the client. If you are going to decide and try Bach flowers as part of your health plan buy them from someone familiar and trained in their healing abilities.

A beautiful idea is to give a special spiritual space to the Lord, a small temple to honor Him. Mine faces the northeast section of my house. I have heard the north east point is very honorable. Some of the ideas I have on my temple are: three white candles for the Trinity, a prayer shawl, anointing oils from Jerusalem, my father's purple heart from World War II, my mother's cross from Slovakia, and my Bible.

I am a Reiki II Okuden and find Reiki to help in the elimination of stress while in hospice. Reiki is the "Universal Life Force." It is another form of healing rediscovered in Japan by Mikao Usui in the 19th century. This loving energy flows where it is needed and benefits your emotional, physical, and spiritual health. Reiki is excellent in relieving pain, balancing energies and chakras, clearing toxins, strengthening the immune system, as well as other benefits to the person. I highly recommend it as a complement to other forms of treatment. It is offered in many hospice facilities.

Acupressure...

It is called contact healing, and acupuncture without the use of needles. Acupressure restores the normal flow of energy, chi. This is done along the meridians. This is done along the meridians. This is done through finger and hand pressure. This is a safe procedure and is noninvasive in nature. Individuals can be taught methods to control pain through finger pressure.

Additional Holistic spa services...

I totally believe I holistic spa services for both relaxation and a promotion of healing through various techniques. I love various types of massage, because I do feel it helps tremendously if done on a regular basis. The circulation of your body can also be helped at home by dry brushing the skin after a bath or shower. Additional services are:

Biofeedback-This is a technique using electrodes connected on your skin, or done through meta-space and using a biofeedback machine. It helps with a variety of health problems including the reduction of stress.

The Bio-feedback that I recommend and have used is Bio-Harmony4Life. It relieves physical, mental, and emotional stress. You can look it up on the internet.

I believe in castor oil packs as recommended through the Edgar Cayce Institute. It is excellent for the lymphatic system. The packs are positioned over the abdomen and help with inflammation, congestion, constipation, and disorders of the pelvic, kidney and liver. They can also be positioned on other parts of the body for detoxification. In the Mediterranean area of the world this is considered the oldest folk medicine. It is called, "The hand of Christ". This can be done on a regular basis. Information about this may be obtained from the institute.

Colon hydrotherapy is an internal cleansing of the colon which is professionally done, and provides the benefits of dissolving and eliminating waste products, that are sometimes in the pockets of the colon. It is helpful in maintaining health on a semi or yearly maintenance. It is done by using pressurized water through an instrument more powerful than an enema. I would recommend looking for a professional in your area and looking into it further.

Take C.A.R.E. for good advice on maintaining your health. The C stands for circulation. The A stands for assimilation. The R stands for recuperation. And the E stands for elimination.

Chakras

You need to keep your chakras in balance. Bless them all and do an exercise to connect yourself with the Divine and all down your chakras into the root chakra or Earth where we live.

Crown Chakra-Bliss-Violet

This chakra is associated with the Divine.

Third Eye (Brow)-Intuition-Indigo

This chakra is our connection with our conscious and subconscious with the Divine. The Divine lives within us.

Throat-Focus-Sky Blue

This chakra is associated with the lungs and throat. We need this clear so that we are not afraid to say words.

Heart-Love, Green

This chakra is for the heart and arms. It is for love and acceptance. Love yourself first.

Will-Power (Solar Plexus)-Yellow

This chakra is for receiving and the broadcasting of emotions. It is also associated with the liver and gallbladder, the nervous energy. The liver is affected by emotions.

Sacral-Creativity-Orange

This chakra is in association with fear, worry, and ulcers. This chakra shows us that love making should be beautiful. It states the women are the ones that bring life into the world, and men are the protectors and providers. Also associated with the kidneys.

Root-Vitality-Red

The root chakra is our fight and flight chakra. And the chakra associated with family and home. It governs all the chakras. This chakra is for grace, forgiveness, and attraction. It is associated with the digestive system.

I Love To Walk With You My Dear

I love to walk with you my dear,
    You bring to me, so much cheer...
Always talking and bringing me a smile,
    That will last mile after mile...
It's fun to tell me about the trees,
    And how I get splashed with mud on my knees...
The lake is beautiful to hike,
    Perhaps the cement, whatever you like...
I'm happy to have you walk with me,
    When we are together we'll find ourselves under a
    tree...
SLB

My Favorites Are Pretty Easy

My favorites are pretty easy to understand,
    If you ask me sweetly, I'd sing in a rock band...
Take me for a round of golf, hope you make par,
    Later in the evening; having a nightcap at a
    sports bar...
I love a beautiful walk by the ocean shore,
    Reading good books, and learning new things,
    never a bore...
Take me for an iced coffee, or any special treat,
    Never be wrong so go ahead massage my feet...
Thinking I have more favorites than favorites song,
    Every day is a new adventure, farewell and so long...
SLB

I Could Kiss You All Day Long

I could kiss you all day long,
    Play me any melody; I'll break into a song...
Giggle we will as we ride on your bike,
    Later on that day to the woods for a hike...
Being with you brings me tenderness, because I care,
    Wishing many happy times for us to share...
Kissing and hugging has been a special treat,
    Enjoying life everyday doesn't that sound sweet...
So save me a stroll down by the shore,
    You know me so well, I'll ask for more...
SLB

To See The Absolute Beauty Of This World

To see the absolute beauty of this world,
As suddenly spin into my existence,
Enchanting music whispers to me all day,
Dancing cascades me, yet allowing me to play,
Life has renewed itself into a new meaning,
Signs and miracles draw near, toward God I am leaning,
Love has been surpassed, by knowledge from above,
Bring forth such devotion, a new meaning for a dove,
For this love cannot be measured in a simple way,
It is so powerful, it truly is meant to stay,
I love this angel with all of my heart,
I know I loved my angel from the start,
I must realize, this I must face,
I can sum up his existence, he is full of grace...
SLB

Life doesn't have to be in Paris, Salisbury is just as beautiful. A beautiful setting, a lovely brook outside to hear the water so soothing against the rocks, and the smell of fresh tomatoes or the planting of a garden. Picturesque, yes life is so beautiful, live it and enjoy.

Animals...

Somehow animals give peace and purpose to a life. Their extraordinary way they give us love opens up our hearts and makes everyday more enjoyable. Look also at the birds that fly in our mists and give our world such wonderment. Remember this: birds meditate to balance out the world that they live in. Go to the zoo, go to the park but go out there and interact with our best furry friends.

Molly

Molly is a sweet little Yorkie, I will always hold dear,
  When I play with that sweet little angel, away goes
  fear...
Her eyes look up as she bends her head to say,
  I'm here to make you happy along your hospice
  stay...
We can cuddle or I will give you sweet kisses on your
  face,
  Throw me one of my many balls so I can race...
Remember every day I'm here just to give you joy,
  Walk me, pet me, I'll be just Molly bring me a toy...
SLB

Rose

Rose you have no idea what love you have brought,
You are a pitbull with the friendliest personality I've
    sought,
You look and greet us with joy all abound,
Wagging your tail so excited, watching it go round,
It's your eyes that communicate with a stare,
Asking for treats from her family cause we care,
Oh Rose you don't even realize what a big dog you are,
You take up the entire back seat of my car,

Lying on your back you give us your paw to say hi,
You follow me around all day, baby Rose why,
You're still a pup just eighteen months old,
I'm wishing you a life of joy ready to unfold,
You deserve to be spoiled with that smile,
Come over anytime I'll walk you an exciting mile,
We can start of brisk as you begin to run,
Oh sweet Rose in all of our lives you have caused
     such fun,
So jump on that window and wonder where we are,
We went out for an errand, never to far,
Rose please remember in your special way,
Keep us company with your smile each and every day...
SLB

Elephant Ride At Busch Garden

We can go on an elephant ride at Busch Gardens
   one day,
      Or perhaps see the giraffe at the zoo, hurray...
See the zebra out our back gate,
      Go to Monkey Island, don't be late...
Did you see the sea lion on Clearwater Beach,
      No, just a palm tree, I wanted a peach...
Seeing a cute frog, so very good,
      Catching a birdie stuck under the hood...
Happy we are together, just spending time,
      Seeing the cute animals, without spending a dime...
SLB

Every Time You Think Of A Hummingbird

Every time you think of a hummingbird, think of our
friendship,
   Their rapidly flying wings of 15-80 times per second,
   Never allows them to trip...
They hover in mid-air, and backwards do they fly,
   About one year for most, three four for some and
   then they die...
They live in South Alaska-Tierradd Fuego in the
Caribbean,
   Migrating south in the fall, if you care to lean...
At night they enter torpor, a sleep to reduce need for
food,
   They have the highest metabolism of any animal,
   always in a good mood...
The flowers they pollinate colors of red, orange, and
pink,
   They hover mid-air rapidly, you'll miss it if you
   wink...
Bee hummingbirds are the smallest birds in the world,
   I know,
   Males are brightly colored, but females have a
   green glow...
They deeply go inwards to pollinate the flowers,
   And enjoy its wonderful nectar, as you and I do
   springtime showers...
So remember your love when the hummingbird will
hover,
   I will, my sweetheart will always be my lover...
SLB

You Love Me More Than Your Favorite Hummingbird

You love me more than your favorite hummingbird,
     When I whisper to you a tender word...
You love me more than the most beautiful rose,
     The fragrance ever changing, upon your nose...
You love me more than Vermont captured in the first
     snow,
     That touch so softly, upon you, that you just know...
You love me more than Santorini Island,
     My smile when you take me to play in the sand...
You love me more than Maybrice Griss Mill,
     Even when my words give you strength still...
You love me more than every sunset, that we did share,
     Even holding me closely, as you touched my hair...
You love me more each day as you understand me more,
     Even though your eyes, shall beauty to you pour...
You love me more, as I too this feeling share,
     Even my darling, remember we are a perfect pair...
SLB

Oh Pretty Little Hummingbird

Oh, pretty little hummingbird, come to see me today,
    Remind me of my love, it is he I long to lay...
You are beautiful and a sight of delight,
    As my angel, he too shall I long for this night...
He loves to see you flutter so free,
    As he does his eyes, when he looks at me...
So come to me kindly, and stay with me if you can,
    You're beauty and peacefulness fills the heart of
    my man...
So magnificent a creature God has made,
    Touching my angels soul and coming to his aid...
Fly lovely hummingbird, always please shine,
    Putting smiles on his face, so very fine...
SLB

Three Little Wood Stocks In A Row

Three little wood stocks in a row,
    One had green, one had blue, and the other had a
    red bow...
They all came out to wish you, a Merry Christmas day,
    They hope your wishes come true, okay...
They are like the wise men, one has a candy cane,
    One has a present, one some food, and one is riding
    a Great Dane...
God bless you and your wood stocks all three,
    Merry Christmas to all, they just went up the tree...
SLB

Games, Books and Movies...

One of the best things in hospice were the Bingo games; however they had bowling, dominoes, and board games. Smiles magically came. Everyone was laughing and enjoying themselves and life was suddenly good.

Hospice provides new movies both in the room as well as the theater. They also had fun locations set up where popcorn or treats were also served while enjoying a movie. Movies provide a nice retreat from reality even for a while. I was told once they are the perfect escape, because for two hours you are magically put into another world to live, laugh and enjoy.

Memories Are What We Need

Memories are what we need,
    Brightening up our days, indeed...
From shopping to finding a special gift,
    To sailing on the sea, and we did drift...
Picking up iced coffee along the way,
    Sea World was fun last Wednesday...
Movies we could pick out for night,
    Sometimes a stroll to see the moonlight...
Wiener schnitzel gave you something great to eat,
    I love massages especially my feet...
Grouper you decided became your favorite dish,
    You loved my cooking especially fresh caught fish...
Remember...
Memories are what we need,
    Brightening up our days, indeed...
SLB

You're A Blessing

You're a blessing that I was given,
　　Making everything in life worth livin'...
Every morning when I wake, I get a new day to enjoy
　　with you,
　　Blessings throughout my day, cause of you who
　　knew...
Evenings are a pleasure to have with my sweet,
　　Movies, dinner, a walk whatever with you, is always
　　a treat...
Going to sleep next to you, makes me a giggle,
　　Surely you know, our love makes me a wiggle...
You're a blessing that I was given,
Making everything in life worth livin'...
SLB

Don't Forget To Call For A Chicken Dinner

Don't forget to call for a chicken dinner,
  With that and a soda, you'll be in winner...
Then off to a movie for popcorn,
  Onion rings at 2a.m. will toot your horn...
When we get home get some ice-cream,
  That combined with a pretzel, and I scream...
Breakfast time requires a homemade fresh donut,
  Combine that with fries, gives you a butt...
Lunch is an enormous and delicious sandwich,
  You are still hungry, that extra taco made you
  itch...
And don't forget the pickle you bought for a treat,
  Homemade rhubarb and apple pie is very sweet...
Wow, dinner of pizza and fries,
  For desert, how about pudding, no sighs...
Enjoy all of your homemade delicious goodies,
  I'll cook always, after all its' my doodies...
SLB

Here's To Your New I-Pod

Here's to your new i-pod,
    It's not as pretty as my bod...
But it has a calculator, and a clock,
    Don't drop it in the water by the dock...
I-tunes to make your day bright,
    Email and contacts to make everything just right...
Videos or cameras could be fun,
    Wait till you check out maps and weather hon...
I bet you can't wait to punch you tube,
    It does everything but an oil and lube...
You can keep up with the stocks,
    Or order from the store new socks...
Notes make your day so fine,
    So enjoy your new -pod with a glass of wine...
SLB

Books are very important in hospice care. I would recommend you read what you enjoy and pertaining to the subjects that you love. I also would recommend the Bible. Just flip it open and enjoy the passage that was meant for you. I like The Secret, which gives you positive thinking into the abundance of life. It talks about the Law of Attraction the ancient spiritual law. I also recommend A Course in Miracles, for giving one hope. This gives something beyond what you dared to ask for.

Hospice is very gracious and the people there do become your friends. It is a home away from home. Your dear friends will come to visit, enjoy them. They may feel uncomfortable but suggest places or activities to put them at ease. It may lighten your heart as well. My gentleman said this about cancer, "courage for the journey, and hope for the future."

This Prayer I Wrote For You Today

This prayer I wrote for you today,
  To take all of your cares and worries away,
God bless you always,
  Until the end of time,
May you always be graced with,
  Compassion and care,
Good health be yours with no pain or strife,
Never neglect to understand how to share,
  With those who need our hand, because we care,
May we be patient and kind to all mankind,
  And thank God each day for the blessings, he passes
  our way...
SLB

My Darling Let Me Wish For You To Know Only Bliss

My darling let me wish, for you to know only bliss,
   The greatest joy in life, when your grandchildren
   give you a kiss...
For it is your turn to savor,
   Children and Grandchildren are God's greatest
   flavor...
Love them and give them your best,
   Until you are so tired you beg to rest...
To them you have been real, kind, and strong,
   They know you would do no one ever any wrong...
So God bless you and your family today,
   Go out and enjoy life, hurray...
SLB

Friends and Family...

The miracle in my life is that I have such wonderful friends. Friends tend to put the person in need first. As many people as you have in your life be grateful. Accept the blessings they give to you and send blessings back to them. The simple fact of sending blessings will enrich your life.

Always live the Smile. I want you to smile at your friends. If you smile you usually get one back. Be aware of how it makes the person happier to see your smile.

Beautiful Smile

You have a beautiful big smile,
   It dazzles me and the sparkles are seen a mile...
Darling, it's the little things that you do,
   That causes me to sizzle, drizzle, and cue...
You're my best friend, I'm so glad,
   With you sweetheart, how could I ever be sad...
SLB

When you pray, say thank you to all those who came before you your ancestors, your family. They made you who you are with their DNA. Everyone on this Earth today- our brothers and sisters are related somehow to us. We have a connection to all. We are interconnected with each other. It is the human element. We are connected to all that God created. This includes all of nature as well. My best advice is to respect all. Thank you and May we all be blessed by Our Creator.

Total Love...

If you are blessed with a loved one cherish it. Tell the Father in heaven to bless them all through the day. Life changes with an illness. Communication changes because it becomes a matter of thanking God every time you receive a call, text, or email. The gratefulness is far greater than can be explained. Suddenly nothing seems important, the clothes they wear, what you are doing, wheelchairs, whatever. It all falls down to one important fact, that person is there for you. Love is the greatest gift and the fact you can share time together. You still have precious time, which is a beautiful gift.

Remember you are exactly where you should be at every moment in your life. Wherever you are, whatever you are doing is learning for your soul. If you understand this one principle, all the suffering, all the drama that you endure seems easier to accept. When two circumstances collide it probably is a learning experience for all. Every soul has his own life circumstances to learn. Remember and respect every person is unique and each is there for a particular reason. We live and interact with each person in our life in a unique way.

Whoever and whatever the Lord puts in my path every day is what I'm supposed to do. Just something as simple, as a smile may brighten someone's day, and they in turn might brighten the lives of others. Simple complements make people feel special. Whatever I do, I will smile, complement, and make others feel special. I will be an ambassador in Jesus' name, and do the actions he would do. I will be the best person I can be. Through continued prayer, I will, and that certainly will make my life wonderful, thank God.

The Most Beautiful Thought

The most beautiful thought,
    That ever crossed my mind,
    Our two lives together, shall we bind...
Never feel less of what you are,
    For me, you are and always will be,
    My shining star...
As I look toward the stars and moon at night,
    I see your beautiful face, in our moonlight...
You have had such a rough ordeal,
    Don't worry, no one else has my heart,
    Or it can, someone else steal...
I am with you in sickness, you're my best friend,
    Together we will fight it, till the end...
With God we shall pray, as we were taught to do,
    When you are here, we will meditate,
    By saying five Hue...
Love, don't be distraught, don't be down,
    I need to see a smile, not a frown...
We will hold on to each other,
    And get through each day,
    After all we were given a challenge,
    Let's show them our own way...
SLB

It is not just the patient but also the person who stands by the patient 100%, this person should also take good care of themselves physically, emotionally, and spiritually. Giving but also receiving love still from both sides of the equation.

My Guy

My Guy is so Humble and True,
    The only one that knows me on cue...
He's taught me many things, oh,
    The word of God, I must know...
He's patient with me, makes me laugh, what a find,
    But best of all, he's never been unkind...
He's a rare jewel, and he is mine,
    Justifiably allowing me to shine...
Hope and inspiration he gives, he does care,
    Sweet ecstasy even with the burdens I bare...
Contentment he gives, my smile does glow,
    Bursting in song, making love easy to show...
In life we pay a heavy price, thus,
    I've paid a price to keep you, it is the two of us...
SLB

We're In This Together

We're in this together, forever my dear,
Closing your eyes, connecting-wipes all fear...
Holding on to options, there is hope,
Love is so special, wasting no time to mope...
Ask for that miracle to come one special day,
Beginning with contemplation, let's begin to pray...
Good Lord protect and make healthy, this man,
Loving and worshipping You, the best we can...
God knows how truly much I love thee,
Praying solemnly, down on my knee...
Jesus said, your choice, my perfect dove,
Remember-faith, hope, and charity, but the greatest is
    love...
SLB

My gentleman wrote this poem for me, and simply called it "Sherri"

I will honor him by including it in my section on love.

Sometimes those that are ill express themselves with love and dignity and grace.

I told him how lovely an expression of love to make me a poem.

> My sweetheart, my baby,
> Is such a perfect lady,
> She loves me with her whole heart,
> Because she is so smart,
> Her truth is so great,
> That no one can take,
> What of her beauty,
> It's all natural and never a duty...
> Bill

I Want To Hold You All Over

I want to hold you all over, to ease your pain,
To erase from your memories, all sickness and sorrow,
Let me bare it for you, at least until tomorrow,
Come close as I touch, and instill your fate,
Tiny touches of love, shall pacify your heart,
If not forgotten, renounced for a while,

I want to hold you all over, to ease your pain,
Let me take it upon me, come close as I whisper,
Release all your hurt, suppressed though it may be,
Let only pure energy flow in thee,
Surround your heart with mine,
Let me hold the burden you bare,
Though it may be not forever,
At least while we share...
SLB

You Just Knew

You just knew...his name makes you shine,
  His lips oh, so very divine...
And his touch sends you places,
  Never remembering, only traces...
The stars appear to be brighter,
  Your step, on clouds is lighter...
His whisper captivates you,
  His eyes so truly blue...
Enchantment by the sea,
  Evoked by passions of you and me...
As the water slowly rolled in,
  Thinking of him, your head would spin...
Your star his saving grace,
  This destiny our eternal place...
He counted every grain of sand,
  As he pledged love; kissing your hand...
His mermaid, this girl would be true,
  He would know; she was you...
She would glance out at the sea,
  Her true love, allowing her to be free...
She would always come back to her man,
  Her heart and soul belonged to this man...
SLB

May Love And Kindness Be Always What Reminds Me Of You

May love and kindness, be always what reminds me
    of you,
    May all the love and compassion, for others always
    shine through...
May your days be as long, as you work need to be done,
    May you always find time with family and friends
    for fun...
May you grow in spirituality, as I understand is your
    will,
    May you process it thoroughly understanding it
    still...
May the Living Master guide you, as best he can,
    May you understand, you are here as a
    human man...
May God's grace continue to keep you whole,
    May you seek deep inside, knowing you are Soul...
May you always find a place giving spiritual love,
    May I walk in your path, always beside you with an
    angelic dove...
SLB

Bravery is the capacity to perform properly even when you are
scared half to death...
SLB

Chapter 4
Spiritual Help During Hospice

Live as if your prayers to God the Almighty are answered...

This is absolutely essential, perfection through God, Our Dearest Father from above. What could be more perfect, nothing, pray it does help. It calms the senses and turns us inward to our connection with God. People who are at the end of their lives tend to want to go inward to reconnect with their spiritual side. I am saying because you are born into this Earth through a deep connection with your God before birth so it makes perfect sense to reconnect with God before death. You will understand your soul through prayer and meditation.

Spiritual Help During Hospice

Heal Me Lord

Heal me Lord in ways still not known to my being,
Allow me freedom, to express my concerns,
Courage to carry them out,
With dignity,
Strength,
That you alone give to us,
Through prayer, meditation, and quiet,
Allow me to heal Lord,
Whether it be,
My way or yours,
Give me full acceptance,
With grace,
That if it be not of this world,
I show acceptance to those around me,
That when I leave,
They show acceptance,
In the Will of God,
And knowing God is the great I AM...
SLB

Whether these be your last moments, or just the beginning it is important to be thankful to God. Thank Him for everything he has bestowed upon you, whether it is good or bad. Everything has a purpose and you will have had spiritual growth. God allows you to understand hospice. People who work in hospice are kind souls.

Father in Heaven,

We ask your kindness and compassion to all people in hospice.

Guide and protect the wonderful souls who help us while in hospice.

Help all those who cross their path every day,

and bless their own families as well.

Asking this in the One most Holy, Your Son Jesus Christ.

Amen.

SLB

What exactly happened at the Cross? Our Lord and Savior gave up His life so that we could have eternal life. Jesus was on the cross and it is to that we lift up our faces in awe of what He truly did for us. When we worship Him who gave us His all, let us make the sign of the cross in remembrance for His Sacrifice, Our Faith, and the Healing if it is God's will we wish to receive.

Father, Hold Me

Just as my Earthly father,
I ask, Father hold me,
With wide hands stretched around me,
Feeling Your love,
Pour healing,
Your spiritual healing inside my body,
Your holiest of Spirits,
Your divine Grace,
Penetrating my essence,
As I give myself freely to Your Will,
And as I contemplate,
This fate of mine,
We call Death,
Let it be peaceful Lord,
Take me fast,
Do not allow my body to linger,
In pain---
For I fear,
Disrespect---
Of not just myself,
But my feelings toward You,
Keep me focused Father,
Hold me close,
Let me sit upon Your lap,

As the whole universe goes around,
And You concentrate, just on me,
Your child---
For even one moment in time,
Whatever Your Will,
It is Yours to decide,
Do with me, My Father,
As You see to do,
And when it is time to live with You,
Take me quickly, out of this world,
And grant me, Eternity,
To live at home with You...
SLB

The word of God will help. Read the Psalms they will strengthen you through their words. The Psalms were meant to be sung, and if you do sing them put your whole heart in them and feel the magnificence of your connection to God.

Psalm 41
Psalm of the compassionate

Blessed is he that considereth the poor:
The Lord will deliver him in time of trouble.
The Lord will preserve him, and keep him alive;
And He shall be blessed upon the earth:
And thou wilt not deliver him unto the will of his
    enemies.
The Lord will strengthen him upon the bed of
    languishing:
Thou wilt make all his bed in his sickness.
I said, Lord, be merciful unto me:
Heal my soul; for I have sinned against thee.
Mine enemies speak evil of me,
When shall he die, and his name perish?
And if he come to see me, he speaketh vanity:
His heart gathereth iniquity to itself;
When he goeth aboard, he telleth it.
All that hate me whisper together against me;
Against me do they devise my hurt.
An evil disease, they say, cleaveth fast unto him:
And now that he lieth he shall rise up no more.
Yea, mine own familiar friend, in whom I trusted,
Which did eat of my bread, hath lifted up his heel
    against me.
But thou, O Lord, be merciful unto me,
And raise me up, that I may requite them.
By this I know that thou art favoureth me,
Because mine enemy doth not triumph over me.
And as for me, thou upholdest me in mine integrity,
And settest me before thy face for ever.
Blessed be the Lord God of Israel
From everlasting, and to everlasting.
Amen and Amen.

Psalm 81
A Psalm of Asaph.

God's goodness to Israel,
Sing aloud to God our strength:
A joyful noise unto the God of Jacob.
Take a Psalm, and bring hither the timbrel,
The pleasant harp with the psaltery.
Blow up the trumpet in the new moon,
In the time appointed, on our solemn feast day.
For this was a statute for Israel,
And a law of the God of Jacob.
This he ordained in Joseph for a testimony,
When he went out through the land of Egypt:
Where I heard a language that I understood not.
I removed his shoulder from the burden:
His hands were delivered from the pots.
Thou calledst in trouble, and I delivered thee;
I answered thee in the secret place of thunder:
I proved thee at the waters of Meribah. Selah.
Hear, O my people, and I will testify unto thee:
O Israel, if thou wilt hearken unto me;
There shall no strange God be in thee;
Neither shalt thou worship any strange God.
I am the Lord thy God,
Which brought thee out of the land of Egypt:
Open thy mouth wide, and I will fill it.

But my people would not hearken to my voice;
And Israel would none of me.
So I gave them up unto their own hearts' lust:
And they walked in their own counsels.
O that my people had hearkened unto me,
And Israel had walked in my ways!
I should soon have subdued their enemies,
And turned my hand against their adversaries.
The haters of the Lord should have submitted
    themselves unto him:
But their time should have endured forever,
I should have fed them also with the finest of the
    wheat:
And with the honey out of the rock should I have
    satisfied thee.

Psalm 97

The Lord's power and dominion
The Lord reigneth; Let the earth rejoice;
Let the multitude of isles be glad thereof.
Clouds and darkness are round about him:
Righteousness and judgment are the habitation of his
    throne.
A fire goeth before him,
And burneth up his enemies round about.
His lightnings enlightened the world:
The Earth saw, and trembled.
The hills melted like wax at the presence of the Lord,
The presence of the Lord of the whole Earth.
The heavens declare his righteousness,
And all the people see his glory.
Confounded be all they that serve graven images,
That boast themselves of idols:
Worship him, All ye Gods.
Zion heard, and was glad;
And the daughters of Judah rejoiced
Because of thy judgments, O Lord.
For thou, Lord, art high above all the Earth:
Thou art exalted far above all Gods.
Ye that love the Lord, hate evil:
He preserveth the souls of his saints;
He delivereth them out of the hand of the wicked.
Light is sown for the righteous,
And gladness for the upright in heart.
Rejoice in the Lord, ye righteous;
And give thanks at the remembrance of his holiness.

Psalm 86-91 Important Psalms for Spiritual Help during Hospice

Psalm 86 A Prayer of David, Prayer for deliverance

Psalm 87 A Psalm of the Sons of Korah, Priviledges of living in Zion

Psalm 88 A Psalm of the Sons of Korah. To the choirmaster: according to Mahalath Leannoth. A Maskil of Herman the Ezrahite, Prayer in the face of death

Psalm 89 A Maskil of Ethan the Ezrahite, God's covenant with David

Psalm 90 Book IV----- A Prayer of Moses, the man of God, Eternal God and mortal man

Psalm 91

The security of the Godly

He that dwelleth in the secret place of the most High shall abide under the shadow of the Almighty. I will say of the Lord, He is my refuge and my fortress: my God; I him will I trust. Surely he shall deliver thee from the snare of the fowler, and from the noisome pestilence. He shall cover thee with his feathers, and under his wings shalt thou trust: his truth shall be thy shield and buckler. Thou shalt not be afraid for the terror by night; nor for the arrow that flieth by day; nor for the pestilence that walketh in darkness; nor for the destruction that wasteth at noonday. A thousand shall fall at thy side, and ten thousand at thy right hand; but it shall not come nigh thee. Only with thine eyes shalt thou behold and see the reward of the wicked. Because thou hast made the Lord, which is my refuge, even the most High, thy habitation; there shall no evil befall thee, neither shall any plague come nigh thy dwelling.

For he shall give his angels charge over thee, to keep thee in all thy ways. They shall bear thee up in their hands, lest thou dash thy foot against a stone. Thou shalt tread upon the lion and adder: the young lion and the dragon shalt thou trample under feet. Because he hath set his love upon me, therefore will I deliver him: I will set him on high, because he hath known my name. he shall call upon me, and I will answer him: I will be with him in trouble; I will deliver him, and honour him. With long life will I satisfy him, and show him my salvation.

Affirmations on positive thoughts may be said out loud to God. Give your positive intentions to God. Made the intention of good health to yourself and state it out loud and clear to God.

I state my affirmation to God today,
It is my intention to be of good health Lord,
It is my intention to have clarity of mind,
It is my intention to have good physical health,
It is my intention to be of good spiritual understanding,
It is my intention to be of the highest good for myself and God,
This is my affirmation to God my Creator, Amen.
SLB

Each soul in hospice is a beautiful individual, and never has to be alone. This is a gift, and it is called hospice. It is a tremendous support system of doctors, administrators, nurses, social workers, chaplains, therapists, and loving volunteers. May God bless each of them and their families for touching every soul in this beautiful home away from home. What at first looked dark now is light. Where hope was lost, it is found through God. This was possible, and I thank Him with all my being.

You have different feelings in hospice as you do when not faced with it. You develop an understanding, I want everyone to know, it does exist. Love becomes stronger for some. It does not waiver. Love does not diminish, and it might fool you and flourish. Love can flourish and give you bliss. You may feel you live in Heaven while you are really on Earth. You might feel you are floating in the clouds. Protect it, accept it, and thank God for it. Love heals. Love gives you a reason to get up in the morning, and a reason to praise God everyday.

On Bended Knees, I Begin To Pray

On bended knees, I begin to pray,
And ask our Dear Lord and Savior, for one wish today,
One wish that might change, lives for the better,
A miracle I say, I ask from my heart,
A fresh beginning, I would rejoice to see,
I pray each day, from deep my beginning,
For my precious darling and me,
For my beloved, to be given a new start,
He's handsome, so sweet, and very kind,
He's dear to me Lord, as sunshine and water
     intertwined,
A fresh beginning I ask for today,
To levitate, destroy, and get outward all his pain,
To totally erase all trace from his limbs,
Let freedom come sing...
SLB

There could be times when you may have a test from God. The pain may become unbearable as the test of Job in the Bible. God gave us the example of Job. Even if we did not pass the test, we are still worthy of God's mercy and grace. Job was a perfect example, we as humans are never perfect. We may try to be, but none of us are. If we realize that to attempt to be perfect in God's eye, is what He expects. If we try from our heart, that is all God expects of us. Job was the perfect example, we are humans attempting to be flawless. We never will be, but we chose to live a better life, because of it. If you are living alone you may experience worries about falling, hurting yourself, food, laundry, a clean house, so many things might go through your head. The pain may become unbearable that you cannot sit, cannot walk, or simply lay down. You may scream even at God, why are you testing me? Dig deep, in your heart and soul remember God has the answers you do not. Yes it hurts, yes Job was tested, and you are not flunking the test, you need advanced help. Get medical help as soon as you can very strong medicines can help with the pain enabling you to lead a good life, ask for help and accept it. Job was extremely blessed. He had a good life after his testing from God. Job rejoiced in knowing God. That gives all of us hope. Trust, believe, and each day may your strength be better than the previous day. Trust that God just as He gave Job a wonderful life will do the same for you. It truly is a gift. Humbly bow down and thank Him for what He has given. Keep in daily communication for your blessings and graciously magnify His holiest of names.

You may not ask for this pain, and you may not understand why you have it, God doesn't ask. He is God. We are not in charge. We are humble to God. We obey God and love God. It is hard with pain. You ask yourself, will God forgive me. Does he know I was in such pain? Yes, that is why He is God and we are not. He forgives us. He knows all. He unconditionally loves us all. Do your Truth not the truth that belongs to someone else. God will give you the answers; if you ask, in silence there are answers. God speaks quietly, listen.

God gets our attention through suffering. People often return to God when they find that life gives struggles to difficult to handle. Never rebel against God. It is better to accept what He has given us. Use all that we have in an honorable and respectful tribute to God.

No one knows how long anyone has in this life. Choose to understand your condition. Focus on what you need to focus on. Whether that be strengthening of your faith toward God, or enjoying the sunset He gave you. Whatever you do, you at this time are very important to your world. Hospice lets you live your life, because they understand the process. God is in charge of who will go into remission and who will not. Live in a state of grace with God. How wonderful to know and realize it. Love God. Do it totally with no question. Be the person in the corner shouting, I love God. Sometimes we see people who are praising God and we may say why are those people acting that way. They could be angels or messengers from God, and they might be the ones wise above their years. They know God. Talk to them, hear their words and thank God for sending them to you, and let us hope we all find our way back to God.

Thank hospice for showing a new appreciation to life, living, and dying. It is a place to share your thoughts. Perhaps even by helping others by what you are going through. It is perhaps just a speck, but even that may touch the right person, and ignite what they need in their final time on Earth before going to their heavenly home.

Know the Lord and feel Him in your heart. Love Him and praise Him and glorify His name. When you have all these tests that God has given to you, accept them. That is your challenge in your life. The truth is God is a miracle. Your life is wonderful even with the problems He presents to you. He is your Lord and Savior and you are blessed. He rules the Earth, the Universe, all this and ever will be. For that all of us are blessed. This will all be made known after death. This realization is wonderful.

You pray for a miracle, but what truly is a miracle. Is it what you want, or what God gives you. People want a cure. To be spiritually cured is a miracle as well from God. The true belief is a miracle, whether you live in this world or the next. Life on Earth is or isn't but your soul remains. Your one connection with God, and always will be. When you understand that you can handle the situation. The future is always held in the hand of God.

A Sign Arrived As If To Comfort Me

A sign arrived as if to comfort me,
Longing to be by his side,
The Lord came to rescue me...
He riveted me off, in a whirl of haze,
Unbeknownst to me until my gaze...

His hand I took into my own,
Comfort I gave him, from depths unknown...
The Lord came with me, to watch us pray,
And God bless Mother Mary, for she would say...

I will lay my hands upon him,
As you cuddle him so near,
You are so worried, do not fear,
Your loved one will be fine now...

He will continue to fight,
He will be blessed both day and night...
So look for dear signs of comfort from above,
Our Lord and Savior will show you, always His love...
SLB

There is comfort and strength in the singing of hymns. As I witnessed many times with small groups of people from churches would serenade the sick. One of my favorites was Beautiful Savior. I feel if you sing the hymns with the Spirit of the Most High they are truly heard by the Father and received as such.

I have written several small prayers to enlighten your days.

Dearest Lord,
He in His loving kindness,
He who has taught us how to express our love each day,
I touch my heart and go to be by your side.
To give you comfort and peace that is needed at this time.
Amen.
SLB

Dear Lord,
Release all my friends of all expectations.
Release my friends of all obligations.
Let me have balance and serenity in my life.
Let me live with unconditional love toward everyone,
As our Lord taught us to do...
Amen.
SLB

Let the Laws of nature be balanced,
Master my destiny Lord,
For the highest Will of God,
For all concerned. Amen.
SLB

Dear Lord,
Please surround the person that I pray for in your hands. I hold them in my thoughts with the divine radiant light and love of Jesus, take away any negativity from that person and immediately fill the space with the positive love and light of Jesus. Amen.
SLB

Jesus, Holy Spirit, Father,

Surround me, those I love,
With your protection,
Fill my heart hourly,
Daily, weekly, monthly, and
forever and ever.
Amen.
SLB

Jesus,
Please never allow negative thoughts to enter my being,
Allow positive healthy thoughts of kindness to shine through my heart,
Never allow anger to flow in my being,
Jesus provide me with joy in my heart always.
Amen.
SLB

Dear God,
Protect my angel you gave me from above,
I am so deeply, deeply in love...
He needs relief from his suffering from his health,
Please heal him Lord, to us that will be our wealth...
All Glory we give, we love you so,

Bless my angel, heal him, my angel doe...
SLB

God's force allows healing to occur whether this be in the conscious state in which we live or through our subconscious state where we visit during our quiet time in sleep. Our mind, body, and spirit all need equal time to be in a healthy state of being. Ask for healing that you may fulfill the purpose for which you came into this life.

Dearest Father in Heaven,
I ask you coming before you with the deepest respect and adoration, to put upon me with favor to resolve the problem I have in my heart.

Please I ask this resolved for the greatest good of all involved.

Keep love in my heart, and help me to send love to every problem, in order to solve it.

I ask the radiant love of my Creator most high to penetrate my aura.

And go deep resolving the issues of the problems I carry in my heart.

If I need angels may I call upon them daily for all of my needs.

And if my needs be so troublesome I cannot handle them, allow me the privilege to call upon a League of Angels of 10,000 to help me, guide me, and deliver me from the burden laying deep upon my heart. I ask this in the holiest of names,

Your Beloved Son of God, Jesus Christ of Nazareth.

Amen. Amen. Amen.

May these spiritual poems and prayers give hope and comfort...

I Thank the Lord Above

I thank the Lord above,
For all good things I have been given,
He's blessed me with so much,
For this I am so sure,
I'm safe at home and so secure,
For this you can surely see,
Many beautiful things he's sent my way,
The Lord has been extra good to me,
My health it is as good as gold,
I will take care of it, the Lord will see,
But of all the blessings,
He has bestowed unto me,
I am most thankful for all for Thee...
Amen
SLB

Realize the power of one. Let me give you an example, when the clock says it is one eleven, I pause and say thank you. I feel the Trinity in the example of three one's, the pure perfection of the number. Sometimes when you see numbers in sequence or when you are reading the Bible and notice, such as the book of James with nine one's I feel a connection with God. Believe in God, your connection, and have fun next time you notice three one's.

I Am Connected To God

Feel the presence in your life,
Feel the life force that only God provides,
Breath, thank Him with your whole heart for this
    breath,
This breath of life,
Appreciate it Holy, Hallelujah!
Ask that the presence of the Holy Spirit,
To fill every space in your being, bringing forth truth,
    God's love,
You are connected with the Most High,
Hold me Father as I humbly bow down to You,
Filling my being with the wisdom of the ages, We
    are One,
Let me understand as I ask for total cleansing, total
    healing,
If I ask for myself, I ask also for my brother,
For Your love sustains us both, We are One,
Both of us Father, Equal in Your eyes,
As You do for me Lord, do for my sicken brothers,
Send forth Your loving healing in all we hold dear,
As today, I feel the presence in your life,
For-I am connected to God...

The Lord's Prayer the perfect prayer taught to us by Jesus to His disciples in Gethsemane. Amen is sealed in trust, faith and truth. I confirm with my entire being.

It is also of great respect to say it three times, Amen. Amen. Amen.

The Lord's Prayer is the only prayer Christ taught to his disciples. Matt 6: 9-13

All Christian prayer is based on the Lord's Prayer.

It is also very beneficial at the time you are saying the Lord's Prayer, to concentrate "healing" of the person your intention is for. Begin by seeing a white radiant light around that person. Then ask God to put them in the highest love and light of Jesus and to surround them in that cascade of blessings. Concentrate and put the sign of the cross over their body asking for their highest good and all those around them according to the will of God.

Healing Services

Healing services are those which give us

My gentleman told me about a healing service in New York City where many people came to pray for his health in a large circle. While he was standing there with the group of people, God came and said, "Your health is up to me. If you want to live it is up to me." He told the group of people what God had said. They all got in a circle and they performed, "hands" on healing service. This was done on him and a couple of other people. He told me, "This service is in my heart." He said he knows that God is truth in his heart. His mind thinks about what the doctors said about his dying and every other type of fear that comes in his mind. He said while he was lying in bed he asked

God to remove his cancer, and not allow the chemotherapy to do damage to his body. He said God told him to act healed.

When you concentrate on thoughts, you give them power. Please concentrate on positive enlightening thoughts for your best outcome.

Healing has been associated with Our Lord Jesus Christ. The disciples continued on his healing with the laying on of hands and using oils for anointments. There are many types of healings in the healing service. It is beneficial for many people for emotional, spiritual or physical healing.

St. Francis of Assisi said,
"The mind does nothing, but talk and ask questions, and search for meanings.

The heart does not talk, does not ask questions, does not search for meanings.

It silently moves toward God and surrenders itself to him."

John of God...

John of God is the most famous medium on the Earth today. He is a healer. He is very humble about his healing ability and tells everyone that it is God, He is the healer. This is done through a method called spiritual distant healing. I have had it done myself, through John of God. I have also helped others who wished to have John of God help them. Dr. Oswaldo Cruz was the entity who performed one healing. There are several entities who are channeled by John of God for healings. For whatever healing we receive we wish to give thanks to the entities, John of God, Our Almighty God, and all others helping in our healings. We wish to send them as they did us God's Blessings and our gratitude.

Guides, Angels, Archangels, Masters

Rely on your guides to help you. Trust totally in Jesus. Understand guides and angels are within talking distance. God does not leave us alone. Be secure in the fact that angels are with you. Angels are with you to help with the hardest of tasks. Trust God and trust the tests that He gives to you. As humans we must realize we are not always given easy tests. Accept your challenges as a learning experience. We are not always at a situation where we can study God and our relationship to Him without interruption. Life gets in the way. There are a million things to do, so never be upset with yourself, just learn and trust God, and then give it to God. He will guide you through whatever situation exists; you might realize God is carrying you. Accept it without question.

Situations are illusions we wanted to come about in order to teach us. Remember your loved ones are also on a personal journey, and they too are learning. The situation will eventually go away, and another situation will replace this one. Understand that everyone is divine in God's light and we each learn from one another. Respect all your relationships, and know each person is here for a reason. Love them and cherish them, as the Father taught you to do. Go inside to know God. Do not stay on the perimeter, go inside yourself. And remember free will. We have the power in the worst conditions to change the outcome. When we write our life contract, understand that free will; is to be used on Earth, and it can change what we want our lessons to be. Pray to God, it is simple yet has effective words.

Ask for help from the heavens always giving them praise, adoration, gratefulness, and thanks. Be the most polite and show your most holy intentions by respecting them through what matters the most to you, whether it be in the form of candles, soft music, prayers, or quiet meditations. They do wish to help you heal, because your body wants to heal itself. Healing energy through our magnificent angels and archangels, masters, guides, and Saints is achieved through true belief, positive beautiful love energy and blessings from God without negativity being allowed to enter. The dark energies can block what the kind loving positive energies are trying to flow. Call upon Archangel Raphael for healing. Ask the permission of the person you are giving healing energy too. Give permission to Archangel Raphael for your healing as well.

Archangel Raphael,

Oh most precious and loving Archangel Raphael, I call upon you in the most loving and humble manner. I ask you and give you my permission as well as the permission of those that I speak at this time. Surround us with your most perfect emerald green healing light, that it can penetrate my every soul seeking out perfect health for me and those I hold dear, in our mental, physical, and spiritual well being. Do not allow any negative energy to come into my being and release any that surrounds me or can cause us pain. I ask for a bubble of light and love to surround myself and those I love giving them healing energy that is of the holiest vibrational state. This I do ask in the name of Our Creator and Father. Amen.

May these spiritual poems give you clarity in your ever abiding faith...

I Know Your Faith Has Been Tested As Of Late

I know your faith has been tested as of late,
    You understand this was to be your fate...
Salvation and its meaning is still not clear,
    Too many messages from sources you hear...
Jesus gave us grace if we truly believe,
    What about other religions, do they achieve...
Now you are asking if the Methodist religion is right,
    Your truth in your beliefs is having a fight...
The A.R.E. Institute made you question your belief,
    Others also understood different messages, what a
    relief...
We shall all go to heaven and be saved,
    This made you question religion, because you
    always behaved...
So do not wonder, just love everyone,
    Be good to your neighbors, and His Will be done...
Your faith will have changed at best,
    Do not contemplate it, let it rest...
For all our souls will always be,
    Just live a life of peace, faith, and love-like me...
SLB

Beautiful Dove Of Togetherness

A beautiful dove of togetherness was found,
After two lovers kissed from above...
A sign of hope for us was given,
To bring my love health, as we both pray for...
Angels will deliver signs if we see,
It is up to us, to open our eyes unto thee...
Thank-you so much Lord, for all of your care,
I will also take care of Him, its only fair...
My love burst out for him all day long,
It grows oh so much stronger, as we go along...
So bless you for the sign of the dove,
We will always consider it, a sign of our love...
SLB

As I Go About My Day

As I go about my day, to my Savior shall I pray,
    That your health grows forever stronger
    every day...
To carry on your mission, to serve the Lord on Earth,
    And when you reincarnate, carry me to another
    birth...
So we can share together, a lifetime whole it may be,
    Together serving the Lord, my love you will also be
    with me...
SLB

One Miracle I Ask From My Heart Today

One miracle I ask from my heart today,
Bowing down on my knees, as I begin to pray...
A wish so profound, and yet so sincere,
Asking our dear Savior, to lend an ear...
A fresh beginning we would rejoice to see,
Erasing all kinds of strife, pain, and misery...
My love he doth suffer, yet brave is he,
Dreaming of gifts of blessings, we hope to see...
Glancing toward the heavens, oh they shine from
    above,
Angelic voices sing, with messages of love...
Lord, accepting your will, faithful always we shall be,
Hopeful in a miracle, we shall see, we shall see,
Eternal Father and Dear Lord, please let it be, let it be...
SLB

So simple, So perfect. Read it, study it, know it, and understand the Bible. Fill your body with the word of God. The words are powerful; the words help to release emotions. Strength is obtained by reading its words. The word of God, given to us to absorb, appreciate, and accept whatever God gives us. Problems are solved by reading it's messages. It is the word, the message, what gives us Hope. Our battles seem like they can be won, because we were given a gift, and that is the Bible, the word of God, and reading that gives us our Life.

Commit yourself even a few verses a day. Have a Bible handy, so you can open it and read God's word. Church is not an hour a week, to worship God, keep Him in your heart always. Love Him unconditionally. Through Christ you will learn to love others as yourself, and treat others kindly, and this is a wonderful thing, a beautiful gift that only God can give you. Appreciate it and smile show others you care, and the love will come back to you, much more than you will ever imagine.

Read other books or topics concerning God. Remember everything in this world is connected to everything else. Whatever you learn, will benefit you in other aspects of your life.

Keep Jesus in your heart, know that feeling, do not doubt it. When God speaks to you, listen. Signs and being able to interpret them are God's way of communicating to us. Look up to the sky, ask the Lord and listen. Say thank you for the sign, never living in the fear that God is not always with you. Be grateful that He gives you messages, to help you through troubled times. Signs are a way of comfort. Even the best of us can be a doubting Thomas. Never put yourself down. God made each of us perfect. He unconditionally loves us, and is there for us. Believe and appreciate God cares so much for each of us that He gave His only Son to save us.

Sometimes in life, you choose to sit, hours on end discussing your faith, the Lord's word, the Bible. Times like those are precious. Meditation with the soft wind blowing upon you reaffirms God understands our need for quiet time to pray, speak, and grow in God. Feel the presence of God, and allow the Holy Spirit to fill your body, rejuvenate each cell of your body in growth toward God.

Ministers, priests, and chaplains all give us something toward our spiritual growth. Use the words that each of them gives to you. They are all special, and each person gives you a new insight toward the true meaning.

A daily dose of the Bible nourishes your spiritual self, as vitamins do the physical, and a sweet kiss the emotional. Balance is the key word when it comes to health. The Bible, the word of God connects us up to Our Lord and when you feel refreshed, you can face more challenges than you can imagine. The Bible is strength, a rock, so cherish it. It is truly one of the most beautiful gifts God gave us. Get your strength from it, and teach other people to do the same. The Bible is the best book ever written, it is God's message for us.

Pick a page, feel the message. Sometimes opening it up to any page, is the message God intended for you. Learn it. It is there for a reason. Nothing in life is easy. Learning isn't either, but words are powerful, and God's words give strength and your life will be better, more productive, with a purpose you might never have imagined.

The Bible a very important book for many of us in this world, would we take it to an island, yes. It is in virtually every hotel room in the world. In times of stress we reach for it more, remember what God taught us, in times of need and in times of joy. Do not neglect the word when times are good, rejoice in it. God provides many avenues of learning for us, as vast as His universe is, learn to savor each of these for what they are for you, as an individual to grow in God.

You as an individual may need time to grow with God. This is your time. Rest. If you need quiet from people, or relationships ask. They will understand. You need to focus on quiet time, to meditate and go inward toward God. Your relationships will still be there, even stronger. Focus, learn, and understand why you were given this time. Grow in God.

Everything will fall into place, believe and never lose Faith. This is a time you need to be self-centered. Do not let anyone try to take that from you. When faced with months, weeks, or days from death, your connection to God is number one. Be very focused and determined to complete your task. Everyone in your life will understand. Through prayer, answers will come to those around you. Total understanding will take over; so that the person, myself may accomplish my greater awareness, greater closeness to God, and clarity unto the journey they are on. Through careful consideration and enough time and space, and perhaps distance those near the patient can acknowledge their need to have a deeper connection to God.

What a wonderful feeling when God becomes first. Suddenly everything else falls into place. Love is expressed, and everything is clear. God gives you what you need, the basics of life, food, water, shelter and emotional support from family and loved ones. God knows and yes he provides.

When illness strikes independence can be a concern. Especially losing your independence, and people hovering around you might get you upset. Everyone must realize this is normal and because people do care deeply. The patient needs to state that he wants his independence or would prefer help. The dynamics of relationships change suddenly when the diagnosis is heard, adjustments have to be made, so be patient and kind.

The patient should try to be strong for themselves. Pray and the strength will come from Jesus. Jesus will make you feel in control of the situation and you will be blessed. When the Lord is with you all problems can be handled. Just ask and He will be there. He will carry you, when you cannot make it on your own. Make your own decisions as long as you can, it is your life. You are still in control. You are a unique spirit, your own identity, and you make your decisions. You may talk to others and get their thoughts. But ultimately this is your journey. Believe in yourself, your values, your faith. True faith in God will always be the right choice. Do not worry about others feelings; they will understand your decisions. Have faith, be strong and you will be correct.

Know in your heart you are enough for God. God loves all His children. We are perfect to Him who created us. We are all unique individuals, and all He asks of us is to love Him. When your heart is beautiful you are beautiful. See the heart, the soul, of the individual. Say, "I am beautiful, because I am with God". I love my Lord and Master. I humbly pray to Him; and have total commitment, praise, and thanks, and that to me is enough.

Mysterious Angel From My Past

Mysterious angel from my past,
    You-my love, are with me at last...
Mystery school we are united, you and I,
    Never allowing ourselves to say good-by...
My friend, we shall search for answers above,
    Transformed into knowledge, as our lives are full of
    love...
God will provide what you are seeking to find,
    He will increase your wisdom and mind...
Read your scriptures from the Bible alas,
    Put it all together, learning with your class...
Together you shall expand your knowledge from above,
    Together you shall be blessed with Holy Love...
Growth, strength, and happiness shall you abide
    in Him,
    As your spiritual path, shall it now begin...
SLB

Hugs, just hugs. How truly wonderful they feel. Hug yourself and mean it. Hug yourself, concentrate, feel the energy you give yourself. Feel the love, love yourself. Appreciate why you are here. Spread the word of God to others. When you spread love you are receiving love. Hugs just hugs, beautiful feelings of warmth. A true treasure we never take the time to appreciate. In this busy time, this 21st century of computers go ahead and hug someone. It stared at the dawn of humanity and it still works today. Use that energy to heal, whether it be physical, mental or spiritual. All three of these go hand in hand. One works better with the other two coming along. Indulge yourself into healing today, hugs, just hugs.

Don't hang on to your illness. Do not empower it. Do not give it energy. Don't say my___. It is the ___. Do not own it. Disown yourself from any disease. State you want to be well. I am healthy. I am well. Whatever disease I have be stricken from my body. I want to help others in this lifetime, in God's name. I want a second chance. See yourself in the future living your second chance. Thank God for it. Praise God, you have a strong relationship with yourself, and now build an even stronger relationship with your God.

God knows what is in your heart, and God understands your relationship with Him. God is number one, always, no question about it. It is and always will be. Accept it. God is in charge. Let go and let God. We can ask, we can pray, yet remember God is God and His word is The Word.

Understand your purpose in life so that if you are faced with the end drawing near you have a foundation to stand upon. A foundation of faith gives us a total commitment to God. Remember it is God's grace not faith that saves us. In His mercy, however when He saves us he gives us faith, a relationship to His son, Jesus Christ. Knowing God and your relationship with Him, and your relationship with Jesus and The Holy Spirit, and in this you can trust yourself to make as solid decision.

Prayer helps. When you are at your lowest you appreciate the feel, of the Spirit of God giving you substance. A total peace comes over you. I felt this in the meditation room of the hospice center when the beautiful Holy Spirit enriched my soul, I looked up and simply said, thank you.

A strong relationship with God nourishes all other relationships. Healing happens when God is number one in your life. Your family will feel the love you have for God, and they in turn will love you more. When you feel troubled God gives hope. When you have no one to turn to God is always there to help. Awareness of God gives hope in times of despair. It is a wonderful thing love, it is our gift from God. Enjoy it as it was meant to enjoy.

The spokes on a wheel would be a true representation of how many ways there are to God. Many people, opinions, but there is only one God. If there are many ways to get to Him, be appreciative that God reaches out to all of us. We need to just ask and He does not fail us. He forgives us. He forgives us for all our sins, because of grace. Fill your body with God's grace, and feel your sins totally washed away from your body. You are free of sin. Your Savior died so that you could be saved. We will go to Our Maker, go toward the Light. God loves you more than anyone else.

Church has to have meaning. It has to move you. You have to be able to tell people why you attend. You feel the message of God, and you feel it. When you get the message from the Sermon, and this doesn't happen all the time, but when you do, it is amazing. Fireworks exploded and what you need to learn at that particular time came into being. God works in mysterious ways, we don't know when the message will hit, but it will. Listen quietly and absorb the word. You will feel the growth inside of you.

You need the nourishment of God's word. It will build you spiritually. I have studied Edgar Cayce, metaphysics, and many denominations and I truly believe God gives you many ways to Him. We all fit in in some way. As long as we get back to God and His way, we are on the right path. Trust that God will give you the knowledge you need at every point in your life, to learn what you have to for your personal growth.

May The Living Master Help

May love and kindness be always what reminds me
    of you,
    May all the love and compassion, for others always
    shine through...
May your days be as long, as your work need to be done,
    May you always find time with family and friends
    for fun...
May you grow in spirituality, as I understand is your will,
    May you process it thoroughly, understanding it, be
    still...
May the Living Master help you, as best as he can,
    May you understand, you are here at this place, as
    any human man...
May God's grace continue to keep you whole,
    May you seek deep inside, and know, you are Soul...
May you always find a place near you to understand love,
    May I walk in your path, beside you, as your angel
    dove...
SLB

This could be considered a poem that is perhaps silly, but with laughter and humor and good intentions Our Lord knows what is in our hearts, and I do produce light cheerful messages as well. Laughter is very healthy especially for the internal organs. It is said it is like a massage on them. People who were very sick watched funny movies for days and constantly laughed were known to do a lot of good for them.

God Grants Miracles And Gives Us Hope

God grants miracles and gives us hope!
    Making everyday easier to cope...
Praise the Lord, give me an amen!,
    Thank Him for blessings each night at ten...
God is Our only God, Jump for Joy!,
    Make sure to share the message with every girl
    and boy...
Hallelujah! Praise! And Rejoice!,
    Glory to God! Shall we lift up and praise Him, with
    our voice...
God is good! Let us praise Him, and sing a song,
    Sometimes so grateful, we'll sing all night long...
God is great! Thank Him for everything,
    We are both blessed, and carried on an angel wing...
Faith will help us, God watches us from above,
    Everyday giving us His everlasting Love...
SLB

Blessings Of The Spirit

Blessings of the spirit,
    Wow! Can't you hear it...
Make a joyful noise!,
    Wow! Strike a beautiful poise...
Rejoice in His love!,
    Wow! From heaven His love shines from above...
The Lord will always bless you!,
For every kind act you choose to do...
Because, everything is possible with God,
    Tell me you are a believer, give me a nod...
SLB

This was written in the way it was intended, for the special feeling the Easter season gives to us...

Easter Greetings To You

Easter greetings to you for this special time of year,
  The Lord has come for all to be saved, my dear...
And as you go to service that beautiful day,
  Remember to worship in my own way...
Stay connected and praise, the Lord from above,
  He gave us a very smile kind of love...
Holding you dearly, I dare not go,
  Secretly caressing your heart, makes me glow...
For I wish you the ultimate Easter to savor,
  I want you always to receive a favor...
Good health and love abundant in your home,
  Joy and sunshine be found in this poem...
So enjoy the beauty that spring will give,
  Enjoy my love, our blessings, and please, live, just
  live...
SLB

The practice of using Holy Water or oil for the intention of healing

Holy water is one of the most powerful Sacraments of the Catholic Church.

I used holy water as well as Oil of Sharon from Jerusalem as other oils when I would do continued blessings on him.

St. Teresa of Avila wrote, "From long experience I have learned that there is nothing like holy water to put devils to flight and prevent them from coming back again. They also flee from the Cross, but return; so holy water must have great virtue."

The practice of speaking directly to The Holy Spirit

I pray to God the Father, God the Son, Jesus and The Holy Spirit. It is important for us to remember The Holy Spirit can flow through your entire body giving it the nourishment it needs. I believe in the power of healing through the Holy Spirit, your body is drenched in God's healing light. Pray to the Holy Spirit and ask it to directly flow through every atom, cell, molecule in your body drenching it with the purest essence of God. This is an energy a life force to keep us functioning. In the Old Testament it was called "Ruah" or the Breath of Life. Just as at the beginning of your life you take your first breath, it is as if life appears. That is very significant as your last breath before you cross over. Ask the Holy Spirit to fill your being with its purest form of love.

There are three types of life force important in our lives. The first being the sun, which is very healthy for us to enjoy in moderate doses. The second is air which is best taken in slow deep breathes giving oxygen to our bodies. The third is the Earth, I have mentioned this in another chapter but exposing ones feet to the Earth for a half hour a day is very healthy. It is healthy to lie under trees and go barefoot for walks on the beach or park.

Ask the Holy Spirit for your particular healing. You may ask for the energy of your higher self to connect with the powers of the divine and speak loud and clear of your healing intentions. You may say something like, it is my intent to be healed. I am grateful for my healing. Holy Spirit please flow through my entire being with the highest good for my being. As long as your intention is honest and you are sincerely trying you will be heard. Trust in God and The Holy Spirit of God.

If you ask the Holy Spirit to take control of the circumstance, such as ill health it will with joy. It is as if you are handing your life to God. God do with me as you wish. Your subconscious will be as it should be. If you hand yourself and your healing to God you are giving the control to Him, and that is when you become open to a miracle. The Spirit of God knows what is best for you and has the highest good for all concerned. You need to have full trust in God.

I believe the most important thing to take from this is to have faith beyond. Ask with your whole heart, look deep inside yourself and ask your subconscious to connect to your highest self. Reach out to The Holy Spirit of God and with all that you have truly let yourself be lifted up feeling his strength love and concern for you and your health. Yes I have seen this first hand and yes this is possible with loving devotion to God.

You Have Been Touched

You have been touched, by the holy hand of God,
You have been obedient and ever faithful in your
    deeds,
Your plea for a healing has been heard on the inner,
To that bow down upon your knee and lower your
    head,
Be with gladness your prayers shall be answered,
Study both Psalm 81 and 97; 86-91 for guidance they
    give,
Be ever gracious to Your Maker, that He created you,
Be accepting that life and death to some, is of free will,
And Our Lord God on high, will guide us,
But it is our choice, as God has given us hope...
SLB

She Laid Her Hands Upon

She laid her hands upon,
As the glow of her spirituality shone forth,
Magically-to heal both emotional and physical ills,
For this is not prayer,
But a connection to the Divine, the Universe,
The unending flow of natural healing,
Given to those-that ask,
We are of God, we live in His world,
Healing comes from the One above all,
As her hands reach down to touch,
As she lifts up to the very presence,
That she was created from,
A healing warmth flows through,
Her hands are met by those that guide her,
As God puts what is needed for healing to occur,
She knows her God is a strong part of her life,
And this the Grace of God came through,
In the holy name, of the One Almighty...
SLB

My Dearest Lord,
As I begin my hospice walk,
Always be by my side,
If I cannot walk, do not abandon me,
Carry me in Your most loving arms,
If I look too weak to move,
Lay beside me in bed, cradling me,
And when it is my time,
Be there waiting at the Gate of Heaven,
Welcome me with all Your Love,
For I have come home,
You have always been on my journey,
And now I am home...
Amen.
SLB

Meditation-

Surrender your problems to God through meditation or prayer. There is great energy in meditation. Listen to the gentle thoughts or words you hear. He will answer, if not right away, it will happen. The key is patience. It is a virtue, and one we should all be willing to learn. In meditation open your heart center and get rid of fear, and replace the fear with love.

My love be so, oh quiet,
Meditate my dear,
Ask the Lord to provide,
The calmness so dear,
With such love, I hold true,
Please Lord bring him blessings,
This moment, I ask of you...
SLB

In prayer ask God for what you want, and in meditation listen for your answer. Ask God remember He is in charge. He knows what you want, but you are allowed to ask. Meditate that your future will have good health. And then project thoughts of yourself as a healthy person; living an active life and enjoying yourself. By putting these thoughts out there and not focusing on kdeath. Tell the powers that be, you want to be healthy and enjoying life. After your meditation thank God for your beautiful future, you are planning, and that He is allowing you to enjoy it.

Grace, fill your total being with God's grace. Meditate see your body filled with the words, and the Grace of God. See yourself healthy in the power of God. Life is a mystery, as the popular song says, but life gives us endless ways, that God has provided to try and help our particular situations. Use them all, listen to those around you, and absorb their kind thoughts and good intentions. The Lord provides us with so many ways to challenge us. Use these possibilities, learn, challenge yourself and grow in mind, body, and spirit.

Feel God so much higher, so much richer and help those around you. Opportunities will come to you. When you have a glow around you people will seek you. They will come, you just need to listen and trust in yourself. Ask God to speak his words through your mouth, your writing, or your thoughts. Everything you want will be possible through God.

Meditate daily to figure out all of your conflicts. It will give you a clear mind. Ask God to give you clarity of mind and listen quietly for His guidance. It stimulates your immune system and releases your emotional conflicts. Your mind when in the meditative state can also concentrate on having only positive energy in the body and releasing all negativity especially illness.

A beautiful way to meditate that one friend taught me is to close your eyes and if you are able to get into the lotus position do so or sit very still in a comfortable position. Image a beautiful lotus flower and see it opening up. Now imagine that it has 1000 petals and see each of them slowly opening until you are deep in concentration. This might take at least a half an hour. Use the intention of health growing stronger for you as the lotus flower blooms to its fullest capacity. This is a beautiful as well as a relaxing thought and meditation.

Mantras can be simple or more complex. Hue the ancient word for God is a very simple and beautiful one, simply say it three times and then meditate as long as you would like to. During the meditation process you may wish to think about three things:

1) To grow more Christ like every day
2) To love the Lord you God with all your heart, soul, mind, and strength
3) To love your neighbor as yourself

When you meditate your intention should be pure communication to your higher each day.

The labyrinth is a very peaceful walk to meditate on. Walking while meditating or praying on a labyrinth is a 4,000 year old tradition. This relaxes our mind and allows us to heal our physical, mental, and spiritual self. To begin pause at the beginning and allow your body to inhale air deeply and focus on your prayer or concerns. Walk inward toward the center focusing on your thoughts for two or three complete turns. Pause at the center of the labyrinth to ask for a solution. While walking outward think about the solution to your problem. At the end of your walk give thanks. If you did not get a solution continue to focus and meditate on a solution. This is a very relaxing walk and you may pause wherever you see fit to pause. Be respectful of others while they are walking.

Surrender His will to the betterment of all concerned. God knows what path is right for you. He knows exactly what and where you should be. God is so wonderful that when you seek His truth, yours becomes so clear. Miracles do happen, and the total peace of God, is truly one of those. Three remain faith, hope, and love, and the greatest of these is love from Corinthians 13.

I would recommend from Toltec Wisdom book by Don Miquel Ruiz the four agreements. Although to study them takes time, I would lie to simplify them and let you get a copy of his book.

1) Be impeccable with your word
2) Don't take anything personally
3) Don't make assumptions
4) Always do your best

Here is a beautiful reading from Edgar Cayce 641-6

'Know that the purpose for which each soul enters a material experience is that it may be as a light unto others."

James 5:13-16

Is any among you afflicted? Let him pray. Is any merry? Let him sing psalms.

Is any sick among you? Let him call for the elders of the church; and let them pray over him, anointing him with oil in the name of the Lord:

And the prayer of faith shall save the sick, and the Lord shall rise up; and if he have committed sins, they shall be forgiven him.

Confess your faults one to another, and pray for one another, that ye may be healed. The effectual fervent prayer of a righteous man availeth much.

To have Faith is to believe unconditionally...

Chapter 5
The End, When Death Arrives

I Saw you Breathing

When you left me, and you took your last breathe,
It was as if the wind, the Spirit of God,
Had just blown across the Earth and had chosen you...
I saw you breathing, as I talked quietly in your ear,
You were not supposed to leave me today,
This was not what we promised each other,
My heart will not understand how to go on,

Yet I am left here, I am dealt the card to live,
Somehow you did stop breathing,
Perhaps that is when your chest was still,
And I prayed as your last breathe was taken,
I guess in reality I did feel when the wind shifted,
It was God, so precious in the form of The Holy Spirit,
It was your day, written long before your birth,
Choreographed with the utmost degree of precision,
You had been taken,
Blown across the Earth into the Heavens,
Because on this day, the Lord had written,
It is your time, and you have been chosen...
SLB

When the end is near there are certain things that come upon the person. At times it may be difficult or painful to touch the person. It is at those times a simple smile, a soft whisper, or perhaps just your presence in the room will help.

The last bath I gave him was the night before he passed away, a time I was not aware he would soon be on the other side. He enjoyed the smell of his favorite soap and his freshly shaven face, after shave and conditioned hair. He had lotions massaged into him and he was so content. I would do mini facials on him and he enjoyed it,+ because he would tell me I used my expensive lady spa products on him. What I want to say is enjoy every moment. Of course I did not realize, but looking back and remembering how happy he was gives me comfort as well. Don't rush your time with your loved ones you may never get it back.

I was told something once and I find it comforting and beautiful. You may have a fear of dying before your last breath but after you do the energy of youth is given back to your soul and the fear of leaving is cast away. The moment of transmission in other words you are there and fear does not exist. This is a gift from your Creator. You will be reunited with your loved ones and friends and great love will surround you. At a later time you may have to go into rest if your earthly body had an illness or problem that you need to overcome before reassuming the life you had in heaven previous to your reincarnation on Earth. But such love will not be known on earth. It is unconditional without judgment or anger, it is not of negative form. We are united into the soul group we have been before and it is familiar to us. One important thing I would like to say is your parents always hold your hands. They await their children and have been our biggest supporters on our earthly existence. They love us so much. Call upon them if they are in heaven and they will be your biggest supporters and fans. It is wonderful to know of their love both here and there is as strong.

When you are aware that you have crossed over go through the tunnel as fast as you can. Ask for Angels of transition to help you go home. Once you have made the transition you will be able to come back as a spirit to make sure everything is fine. It is important to remember that. You may also call on Jesus to help. Your loved ones will be there to welcome you back and to help you get readjusted. Your spirit guide is there along with family members to help you as you adjust to your new life. It is a re-orientation to your new life. Sometimes the soul needs energy repair work this is called rejuvenation. It is similar to an energy shower of light and sound, some souls need more. Some souls feel as if they are in a hospital getting much needed rest until they heal. We as caretakers may also ask that the angels of transition or our loved ones to help assist them. St. Germaine and St. Michael also help at the time of death. It is important that you pray for your loved ones at the time of their death that they have passed to heaven and that their energy is restored.

Allow Me The Selfishness I Never Showed Him

He is gone-
As swiftly as you gave him to me Lord,
He is gone,
Last rites, the Lord's Prayer,
Yes, it comes so natural,
But I beg, allow me to stay,
    To remain,
For he is mine,
    Not yours,
His body is still warm,
His soul-the Lord taketh,
But I have his body,
It is still warm,
Allow me my tears,
Allow me my sorrow,
It is ours-
    Between us,
He holds me now, from somewhere else,
His love is here,
    It remains,
Please do not come,
With empty words-
I understand time,
I understand obligations,

I do,
But you, must understand,
Love...
It does more, means more to me-
    Than your time,
    Your work,
I need to stay here,
While it is still fresh in my mind,
His passing,
To feel my beloved,
In the way, I need to feel him,
Do not judge me,
    Move me,
Try and comfort me,
Just allow me To Be,
Allow me to Be,
Because I lost him,
You did not,
If I am selfish,
Then allow me the selfishness I never showed him,
And let me grieve,
Just let me grieve...
SLB

These thoughts are directly to the nurses, assistants in a hospital setting after someone has just passed on. I do not care if you are on a deadline, I do not care if your lunch hour is approaching, this is perhaps the one most important time in that persons' life. Show respect. Actually learn respect. From my perspective you do not hear, care, anything what people are saying to you, you act polite only, because that is how you were brought up. Your heart is torn apart. The last thing you want is someone trying to make small talk to you so that you have to go deep and try to make them happy. This is your sorrow. It has to come out. You absolutely need time to talk to the one that passed, to perform last rites, a prayer or simply hold their hand. You do not need to apologize. This is your loss not theirs. And no amount of schooling can teach that. I was rushed out and I still get angry about it. I was driving around streets lost when I knew my way, because they had told me to leave before I wanted to go. Hospice will tell you take your time, and then come right back at you and say donations have to be made, we need the room, quickly remove everything so we can move on. Move on who do they think we are robots, this was our life, our heart, our soul, so do not leave if you feel you are not ready. I was rushed and I was unable to process the situation fast. Things should not be done on a rushed basis. Do not do what I did, take your time. Remember it is your loss. They should be helping you, not the other way around.

You'll Never Forget

You'll never forget, never forget,
Those feelings knowing-
The ultimate truth,
    His truth,
    He is gone,
To his maker, he returned,
Now I am left,
Half of what used to be complete,
Half of my being is also there,
Rebuild, no it is too soon,
I can barely walk,
    Barely talk to people,
And no explanations, ask,
It does not help,
Unless he comes back,
Nothing you can say,
    Or do,
    Really helps,
It is but-
Momentary kindness from you,
And that shall eventually,
    Turn me around,
But I need time,
    Too much time,
I need love, so real,
And I feel this loss,
    This loss,
I will never forget,
Yet, I do hope,
    I can,
Live without this desperation of feeling,
Like I can never forget,
Never forget...
SLB

His warm body is starting to feel cold, and the once soft touch of his arm is getting stiff. Yes I have had that experience before, but it is never easy. You are numb. You do what you have to. Later on while looking at his picture and thinking of that time, in reality I knew he had already left, but I didn't want to let go.

In An Instant

In an instant the body that I had known is now given
    back to God,
Replaced by your heavenly body of light,
Your body is now free to ascend dimensions forgotten
    by us,
Where we have lived, called it our home, but forgotten,
I hold unto you, but this is not you, it was,
You are the Soul that we both talked about,
The love that will never leave me, but protect me from
    harm,
This earthly body will again become the dust from
    where it came,
And your Soul will be free to float high above us all,
I close my eyes, trying to imagine this newness,
For you are truly happy, no pain, contentment,
All our loved ones gathering to greet you, as you
    are now,
As my eyes do close I feel peace, for that is your
    uplifting,
And as I open my eyes, I see your picture,
The man that I cannot touch anymore, that perfect
    creation God made,
That I knew, so well, has been taken and given his
    freedom,
His body that my picture shows, is no more,
He is an angel, my angel, and shall always be,
For our lives, his life was changed,
In but one minute, in an instant...
SLB

The first hours after I came home from his death bed, I do believe I was in total shock.

I wrote this note on my kitchen table. "I have nothing. In having nothingness, I will find something."

The days following the funeral can be a total blur, not fully understanding how you are even getting from room to room. I could not walk, absolutely no energy. I did not want to find words to talk to people yet the words somehow formed and I was released of feelings to strong to fight. The first day I barely made it to the mailbox, and my son a doctor told me you have to just go a little more each day. I remember getting a few houses away and so proud of myself. I worked on longer and longer walks it was not my endurance it was mentally I could not focus. Grief works in many ways not eating, talking, moving, everyone is different, and all should be respected. Everyone accepts things a little different. Eventually I told myself I was going to walk for a purpose. I would dedicate my first half marathon to him, I was somehow getting through my grief. if I could actually do it. So I walked and walked and walked and I did it, I finished in great time much to my amazement.

You Touched Me Sweetheart As No One Else Can

You touched me sweetheart as no one else can,
Your love let me embrace, and hold it dear to
    remember,
The truth of your quiet words,
The wisdom of the thoughts you have,
The kindness of your heart,
Your loyalty to those you love,
There can be no other, in this world or another,
That has brought such blessings and hope,
My sweetheart, how can I ever forget,
You touched me deeply, as no one else could...
SLB

The funeral can be either loving or stressful. Unfortunately at times of funerals if there are step-families involved many times some of us are left out. I suffered the greatest loss of my life and went through the funeral by myself, because the family that did support me was out of town. Believe me it can be done. I do believe looking back on it he must have carried me on angel wings. I was in shock with a broken heart, not that I even knew I still had anything resembling a heart in me. There I was at the single worst moment of my life sitting by myself in the second row of the family section totally raw, the hurt so bad it could have been cut with a steak knife and I would not have felt a thing. I sat motionless, breathless, without a word to come from me yet asking God how could this be? He should have been next to me. We were at a friends' funeral three weeks prior. What did I do to deserve this? I was all alone, and stripped of the one person in this world that I could not live without. So yes is the answer to all of you out there, yes it can be done. If I could go through it you can. If I could attend the funeral of my better half all alone totally starting over with nothing in my heart, yes it can be done. Hopefully I can help you in later chapters. God must have been there. He must have sent every Angel, Archangel, Master, Saint, Spirit Guide from both mine and his side to hold me spiritually, because I made it. Somehow the words of the prayer came through and somehow I would learn to live again. By the Grace of God I did learn to live again.

A Smile On Hold

It is as time has put a smile on hold,
The world knew my smile,
My sweetness that bathed strangers with kindness,
Never asking,
Just giving,
The Lord knows my smile is in heaven,
It has been replaced with nothing,
No feeling at all,
I want to smile,
Deep-
Tell me how,
If you are truly my friend,
How do I face the greatest loss of my life,
How do I face that,
And yet face,
The look of what should be loved ones,
Not even comfort expressed toward me,
Do they not know,
     Understand,
Torment,
     Pure, real, unmatched,
Torture that is tearing,
No-torn my heart into 1000's of pieces,
And yet,
I receive nothing,
No hugs, no sympathy,
I sit alone, by myself,
Holding what little of myself I have together,
To make it to a life I don't even know exists,
But alone,
Totally alone,
I sit,
Except with the one who is now in heaven,
He is here,
I feel he is here...
SLB

He was called unto God, and if I shall remember to be humble to God, who am I to question God. If I put God first then everything will fall in place. I need total trust and belief. Life has a way of testing us in ways we may not want. It is our responsibility as children of God to accept the challenges he gives us. Knowing we are growing in our spiritual dimensions. Embrace the challenge that God presents to you, as a learning experience. I remembered from our long discussions on God, "keep an attitude of love for the obedience to God." In other words, God is ultimately in charge, Obey.

He Cries With Me

He cries with me,
Tears sprinkling down upon me,
First as a gentle rain,
Later as a storm,
He feels my sorrow,
For I am not ready to say good-by,
I miss him, I want him back,
In whatever shape God gives him to me,
Yet, I am faced to mourn,
Wanting others to be happy,
Please, not myself,
I need to cry,
I need to mourn,
I need to own my sadness,
Feeling every inch of pain,
Through every part of my body,
Deeply, hurting---
Before I can heal,
So allow him Lord, to cry with me,
For he knows my heart,
For it is his soul that lives in it,
As he cries,
In his home in heaven,
He sees his love,
Desperate,
Sorrow flowing,
And his tears are shared with mine,
A crossover of concern, understanding,
And love,
That my tears and his shall be,
A healing to both our souls,
That his life and mine, continue---
Mine in this world,
His in the next...
SLB

I found comforting thoughts in my father's Bible after his death, this was one of them. Unfortunately no author was mentioned.

When I come to the end of the road,
And the sun has set for me,
I want no rites in a gloom-filled room,
Why cry for a soul set free?

Miss me a little, but not too long,
And not with your head bowed low,
Remember the love that we once shared,
Miss me and let me go!

For this is the journey that we all must take,
And each must go along!
It's all a part of the Master's plan,
A step on the road to home,
   When you are lonely and sick of heart,
Go to the friends we know,
And bury your sorrows in doing good deeds,
Miss me, but let me go...

I have experienced great loss in my life as many of you. One of them came early at age nineteen when the woman my Great-Aunt Julianna Kolesar Parobek who along with my parents raised me, died in a coma while I left the room for a moment. She was the one person who had taught me unconditional love toward all. I remember in my heart I asked God to take me and spare her, and I truly meant it. To experience such love toward another human is rare, much like the love we have for our children and hopefully our spouse. But it gave me a valuable lesson the one person God took had given me her all. I prayed to God to allow her to be with me until I was fully grown, and God in all His glory had done that. I was nineteen years old and God had fulfilled my wish, He had waited to take her until I was an adult. May I say in front of the world, God is indeed gracious and so very kind. Since my early childhood He had heard my prayers and had taken her at age 98. She is still with me and always will be. She had such love for her entire family and that love is still with all of us, for my family is beautiful loving and growing through Our Lord and Savior each day.

My father was taken to his heavenly home after a long illness of 14 years. Through his illness and battle with cancer I learned an important lesson, we may think our time will be up before another, but God truly is in charge. My dear father outlived many that seemed very healthy at the unset of his disease. He was the bravest and most spiritual man I ever knew. He quietly instilled in me such true belief in God by just his quiet presence. His devotion and undying love for God never left him, it only grew stronger. He was unable to eat or enjoy what we all take for granted the last three years of his life, yet in his quiet devotion prayed for all of us on a daily basis. He put the needs of others before himself. I will never forget his total unending love for God, and I do hope in some small way, me and my children will feel the absolute oneness with God the Almighty that my father on Earth did.

My dear mother returned to her maker nine years after my father had passed away. She was of ill health also in her later years with Alzheimer. I remember my dear beautiful mother with a loving heart to all of mankind. She had mentioned to me how lovely that our country had made a holiday for Martin Luther King, because he was a great man indeed. She had absolute love for her entire family and when I attended church with her I learned of her deepest respect for God her Creator. I wanted to follow in her footsteps and I feel her presence with me along side me at mass. I will always miss my mother on this Earthly plane, I am aware she is with me in spirit, but I do long for those days long ago when I could just go to her house have coffee and chat.

I have experienced grief and the end with many of my closest people. Memories are so precious and what the people actually taught us remains. When I come to the end the only thing I wish to have accomplished is that I brought even one person closer to God. For as the Shepherd went to find that one lost lamb, if all of us saved one soul, imagine how wonderful this world would be. Our end would be a reason to celebrate.

Psalm 88
Prayer in the face of death

O Lord God of my salvation, I have cried day and night
    before thee:
Let my prayers come before thee; incline thine ear
    unto my cry;
For my soul is full of troubles: and my life draweth nigh
    unto the grave.
I am counted with them that go down into the pit: I am
    as a man that hath no strength:
Free among the dead, like the slain that lie in the
    grave, whom thou rememberest no more: and they
    are cut off from thy hand.
Thou hast laid me in the lowest pit, in darkness, in the
    deeps.
Thy wrath lieth hard upon me, and thou hast afflicted
    me with all thy waves. Selah.
Thou hast put away mine acquaintance far from me;
    thou hast made me an abomination unto them: I
    am shut up, and I cannot come forth.

Mine eye mourneth by reason of affliction: Lord, I have
 called daily upon thee, I have stretched out my
 hands unto thee.
Wilt thou show wonders to the dead? Shall the dead
 arise and praise thee? Selah.
Shall thy loving kindness be declared in the grave? Or
 thy faithfulness in destruction?
Shall thy wonders be known in the dark? And thy
 righteousness in the land of forgetfulness?
But unto thee have I cried, O Lord, and in the morning,
 shall my prayer prevent thee.
Lord, why castest thou off my soul? Why hidest thou
 thy face from me?
I am afflicted and ready to die from my youth up: while
 I suffer thy terrors I am distracted.
Thy fierce wrath goeth over me; thy terrors have cut
 me off.
They came round about me daily like water; they
 compassed me about together.
Lover and friend hast thou put far from me, and mine
 acquaintance into darkness.

I have nothing
In having that total nothingness,
I will find something...
SLB

Chapter 6
Grief

Love lives on...

This is dedicated to my daughter Suzy, my Rock, during one
of the most painful times in my life

You Did Not Leave Me

You did not leave me,
You allowed me my grief,
Though strict at times,
Your comfort shone through,
Your push, your drive,
To forcefully make myself proud,
Of what I could do,
What I could accomplish,
All the while knowing,
He was here,
Wishing me well,
Helping me from behind a veil,
So sheer,
I could almost see through,
But you my Rock,
Held the faith,
For the two of us,

Your thankfulness was given,
By the gracious thank you from Heaven,
Of being her Rock,
When she needed one,
And someone He could count on from Heaven,
To make sure ma-ma survived,
And so it is...
SLB

The Daughter I Cherish

You gave me hope, you held my hand,
You saw my tears, your heart understood,
My flowers you set at a place of honor,
My possessions you knew I could not disturb,
You sensed my pain, as you as well had grief,
You did not rush this process of loss,
You gave your mother your strength,
You are a true child of God, for you do care,
Always my Rock, as I had been to you,
Never deserting me, as my protector you stood,
Watching me carefully, giving small daily doses of
      hope,
Listening to my grief, that I could not settle,
It was you that never gave up,
You who knew I would survive and live again,
And that I did, you knew the word was time,
You knew the act was love, and that you gave to me,
I gave you love as well, the daughter I cherish...
SLB

We all need one person who no matter what allows us the total freedom to grieve, without judgment. Allows us the luxury of sitting outside in one's car and weep when we come home from an errand or weep when we finished driving and heard a song that drove us to tears, everyone needs that someone. Emotions run so many ways I would attempt to say a circle with arrows pointing a thousand directions. You might think you are all right so perhaps a half a second and then crash hard, so hard you can't imagine ever standing again. My daughter was my Rock perhaps put there at that time and space for both of us to learn. The veil though it is perhaps reachable is just that for a short duration of our time. Yes they do reach out to comfort us through their gestures but it is the rest of the day, that 24 hour cycle unbearable to most of us that have somehow made it through, somehow survived, and somehow owe it perhaps to that person who witnessed it and grew as a person because of that.

Death occurs to all of us as we were always told taxes and death. The hardest thing in life is when death occurs to your loved one. No one is ever prepared, how can you ever know that hurt until you are face with it head on. How do you count the tears until they do not cease. Prepared I read all the books, I tried yet as prepared as one might think they are it hits hard. It hits like a brick coming toward you at one hundred miles an hour. I thought with my deep sense of religious background I would be spared, but grief spares no one. It hits hard. It does not care if you are prepared or not, prayed or not, it hits and you need to know, you will fall. You will fall, the good news is eventually you will get up. It takes time, patience and courage but if I could do it you certainly can.

Matthew 5:4

Blessed are they that mourn: for they shall be comforted.

Proverbs 14:12-13

There is a way which seemeth right unto a man, but the end thereof are the ways of death. Even in laughter the heart is sorrowful; and the end of that mirth is heaviness.

The Angels Saw Her Cry

And the angels saw her cry,
And weep she did,
For all of heaven to notice,
Tears flowing-rushing-down,
As if that only could erase it all,
Comfort-hidden,
It would not cease,
Misery, contemplation,
Knowing-heaven knew,
Life is so short,
So precious,
Why is not every one,
Privilege to that,
Know---
Why doesn't everyone understand...
SLB

I was totally not prepared for this amount of pain, how deep it could hurt, and how long it would last. People try to distract you believing it will help, but you alone how much you need to grieve. I was not prepared for the screaming I would do, the hysterical crying, my thoughts of if I could ever get through this nothing would ever hurt me again. Yet we do not know what God has in our plans for our life. The process He has put forth to allow us growth. At the time of grief you are so engulfed in the process you do not want to carry on.

I Live In A State Of Total Sadness

I live in a state of total sadness,
How do I go on?
Do I want to?
I feel no hope, no justification for this,
I was dealt a situation, I never dreamed of,
Never asked for, don't want,
This unbearable pain,
Even when you were in pain, could never equal this,
We had each other, you were alive,
I feel your presence now,
But it is not the same,
I know you are with me,
My selfishness wants your physical body,
To hold, to touch,
As I look upwards I ask,
Is this all Lord?
Do I have it complete,
Or do I have to be hurt again,
For I do not have him to give me comfort,
He is gone,
For all I have learned, for all I have studied,
Has not prepared me for this,
Unbearable grief, unbearable pain,
That I alone must learn to overcome,
To live...
SLB

There is a point in the grief process you realize death comes to all. No one is guaranteed how long we have. We are born, live, and then return from where we came from.

Death Is Inevitable

Why does anyone have to go through this Lord?
    Death is inevitable,
We most all return,
    To where we came,
But those left behind,
We have uncertainty,
    Of a loss that we question,
With our faith, we still demand-
    Questioning God,
As if it is our right to ask,
Was I not told to be humble to God?
Why do I now cry?
    Cry out to God,
    With tears overflowing,
As swiftly as they came,
Why-where is the fairness?
Did you forget Lord?
    To give me strength,
I crumble,
    On my knees,
    Looking upwards only to You,
For guidance, answers,
And yet, my tears do not allow me quiet,
They wrestle at me,
    Preventing me from functioning,
    Existing,
You say you have every answer,
    To our questions,
I ask why---
    Waiting---
    Seeking your voice,
And all I hear,
    In the loneliness of my room is,
It was time,
It was time...
SLB

Grief does not allow us a normal existence. We go through the motions. I did, I started to eat, exercise and work. I did daily routines but that constant hurt never ceased, I would do my business with a constant pain in my chest. I adapted to the pain, it was difficult to exist beyond what I can explain, but you do it, just because. You have hope that one day, it will surprise you the pain will subside, and gradually hopefully fade into a lovely thought perhaps a beautiful memory. But right now you play the waiting game, how much longer Lord should I suffer, and can you if I ask magically come and take it from me.

This Pain Is So Real

This pain is so real,
I can feel its name,
It is Pain,
I can scream,
So all of Heaven can hear,
I ask, do they hear?
Do they see my ever-flowing cascade of tears?
Why does this not end?
Why does it not cease?
Have I not faced enough grief,
Enough pain,
Go-riddance, please I beg now,
     Go riddance,
I cannot deal with one more moment,
     One more day,
Yet, I must,
In my silence,
To those around I am quiet,
     Serene, still,
Unbeknownst, to them, my pain,
The silence I keep,
Asking only God to hear,
From Him my silence is broken, his ears hear all,
Even though my words are not spoken...
SLB

What happens when a holiday, birthday, or anniversary come along. The memories fill you exhausting you of completing what needs to be done now. Even now two years past his death I find myself pausing silently as if I am staring into the distance. I am with people but my reality is somewhere else. That is normal. It will slow itself down. If you catch yourself doing it after several years that is still normal. My mother has been gone over twelve years and I still find myself wanting to pick up the phone and call to tell her something. Holidays although enjoyable, I do find a missing part. That is when we most look inside your heart and they will be there.

Look Inside My Heart

Look inside my heart, and you will see,
All of my loved ones are still a part of me,
Each has a section pulled together so tight,
It's oh so wonderful feeling perfectly right,
Ancestors I respect and honor all of you,
Praising the Lord above with giving you life, anew,
For in thanks, remembering and giving respect,
We honor ourselves, by honoring you,
I give you my respect, my love, my prayers,
As I humbly look into the heavens,
Where each of you lives with our same Lord...
SLB

While we are going through the grief process we realize things are not right. We accept it and try from the depths of our souls to reach deep within while attempting to pull us back to living, to life...

Not Living A Normal Existence

Not living a normal existence,
I have to pull so deep inside of me,
    To get through,
Cry, Cry, and more tears,
They say tears cleanse,
Then, I have cleansed,
    I have cried,
Yet, it eats me at my core,
No one sees,
I do,
They go about their business,
This life, it does go on,
Life does go on,
I have to somehow fit in,
    Somehow go on,
How, Why, Where,
All the standard questions,
Yet, though I speak to myself,
I have not the answer,
I live without answers,
    Of not knowing,
    Existing,
I eat, because I have to,
I breathe, because somehow,
    Someway, my body does,
But I don't really care,
    If I do,

And somehow, somewhere,
I need to go deep,
So deep,
Tugging at myself,
Just not now,
Let me have my sorrow,
Let me have this time for Grief,
And maybe,
    Just maybe,
Tomorrow I will awake,
And decide to Live,
To Live...
SLB

I Surrender

This deep-seated grief,
Has settled so deep,
I feel it as an entity,
It takes over my being,
I cannot do my work,
I care not for anything,
Yet, I feel-I need too,
Where Lord does this go,
What future exists?
While this grief, so much remains,
My body feels full,
It is engulfed in grief,
So strong, my soul cannot surface,
My feelings cannot be stilled,
    I surrender-
    I surrender-
If that does not give relief,
What chance, can I now be,
My head exists,
Yet pain is so strong,
I give up Lord,
    I surrender-
And even with such pain,
Please just let me-
    Surrender-
    Somehow surrender-
SLB

My Heart Does Not Live Here Anymore

My heart does not live here anymore,
Please God, I dare scream,
    Set it free,
Mine is cast,
As in metal to a heart,
    Asleep,
Caring, yet on such a hold,
Angels, Archangels, I cry out,
    Please help,
I have no other to comfort me,
Searching endlessly at the darkened moon,
    Stars glazing upon me,
As I look up to see familiarities,
Hoping for realization,
It's endless this wait,
The pain continues as if I could burst,
Would it end, and I begin in a new awakening,
A cocoon awaiting-enter,
Into a world yet explored,
But no, I hang on-
    To the hope,
The security I know runs along,
And dare I go back,
Back to a sleep,
A dreamland, where hope exists,
Or just remain a wander,
Where existence is pain,
Reality's name is pain...
SLB

Constant Battle

I cannot keep this up,
Constant battle,
   With my soul,
Release this hurt,
Or must I hold it,
   To know,
   Fully know,
What grief is,
   The definition,
I live it, breathe it,
I do not savor it,
Yet, it runs through my veins,
Clinging to my existence,
Holding me,
Not wanting to leave my side,
I pray, I meditate, I hope,
Desperately for my heart to be healed,
To feel something,
   Anything,
But such hurt,
   Such agony,
   Such grief,
I go about,
   Expressionless,
With no utterance of a word,
For joy is not,
   Welcome here,

I need to feel this,
Live this,
Live this out,
    And deep,
So deep, it,
Reaches my core,
My soul,
I know that if I make it through,
    To the other side,
I call hope,
A new life,
    Might be,
Might this soften this hurt,
While I sit quietly,
As grief holds my part...
SLB

During grief I went through different stages, at times I felt very emotional and wanted so much to reach to the other side. I talked to many mediums connecting me with the other side. Every time I did talk to others in the other dimensions I was so comforted. I would highly recommend it if you need reassurance, but please get someone very reliable, and highly recommended.

I also used nature for my healing process. I used the calm of the majesty I saw at the seashore, while I quietly went for a walk...

Do You Feel Me Darling As I Stand In Our Bay

Do you feel me darling as I stand in our bay?
 My feet touching the sand, oh that you nay...
The magnificent sunset of such shades of pink and
 gold,
 Enchanting my connection to my Creator, I'm told...
As I hear the rush of the waves tumbling down,
 The lights decorating the magic of St. Pete town...
Oh how I wish you could feel me, at the waters' edge,
 Burying deeper my feet, creating a man made
 ledge...
So serene I am at play,
Watching the stars shine,
 For they have appeared quickly, so divine...
So as I say goodnight, and toss my hair to the wind,
 dear,
 Come and feel me close in our bay, so I might
 cheer...
For my heart did race faster as I thought of only you,
 As I look into the horizon, dreaming so true...
SLB

These are the words I wrote after his death, yes I did write-constantly.

I do not know to go on living my life. I need to take things extremely slow. I will bury myself with errands and work, trying to keep my mind so busy, so that I don't have to feel the pain. The pain is extremely hard to bear, as if it were to be seen, a chainsaw not a knife would be required to go through it. I feel for myself even to have a chance, I need quiet. My friends might think they are helping but my heart is broken. It needs to heal. The quiet of prayers and meditation and sleep and the combination of allowing myself the ability to work, hopefully will heal me. I need healing foods, nourishment for my body, because I do not know where to begin. Sometimes just cooking for others is healing. The simplest tasks we take for granted allow ourselves to attempt to move forward.

The truth, the reality nothing really helps. It is something you have to go through. The process of pain so tremendous, how do you cope? You learn to try. You read every book you can get your hands on. You read every book about life after death hoping beyond hope, you will learn to live. I am a woman and somehow girl things helped. It was the makeup, exercising, going to stores to look around, flowers, every possible thing I could do to distract myself. I tried it all but at the end of the day I just hoped I would make it to another day.

Grief is similar to depression. You need to accept your circumstances and make the best of it, not giving up. Believe me I understand how hard it is I lost what I felt was everything, but somehow you pull yourself up and each day a little more and more until we heal. I had no parents to comfort me mine had both previously gone to heaven. I felt like an orphan, but when you are at your lowest you dig as deep as you can go and survive.

It's Gone

It's all gone,
Nothing to give,
   Anyone else,
I have such emptiness,
Compelled beyond-
What I thought possible,
Lord, fill me,
   Somehow, someway,
I know not,
   Even to speak,
Words do not flow,
My pen, my companion,
As if poetry-cures,
But does it,
I know not-
I just write,
To mask my fears,
   Tears,
Endlessly flowing,
Disrupting my life,
Hiding in shadows,
   For none to see,
Underneath holding on to grief,
   Such grief,
I can cut it,
Thick, unending grief-
At what cost,
I dare not speak of it,
For no one knows,
You mask it,
You hide it,
You grieve...
SLB

Sometimes God gives us big problems to deal with at the same time as our loss so we have to live and deal with that as well. You feel like screaming out-I need time, but life doesn't give you that luxury. You are forced to deal with problems unlike you have ever known, and still feel the pain from grief like a knife to your insides.

People Do Not Know

People do not know,
    What lies within,
Hurt, deep from expectations,
    Not allowed to be filled,
Remorse, questioning,
Trusting, a limited few,
For no one knows,
    No one truly understands,
And you don't wish,
    It upon them,
That loss,
    That insecurity,
The total giving upon this world,
Dare I ask you?
Why does my smile,
Have to be upon my face?
Why do I have to laugh, not cry?
Talk, not have silence,
Look to give comfort to another,
When I have none to give,
I need it,
    I scream out,
Yet, no one can hear me,
I scream loudly,
    Inside,
Where my heart,
    My lungs,
    My organs, Here-

But no one others,
I am alone,
　　In this fight,
Only God, is by my side,
And I go,
To the ends of my depths,
Where no comfort,
Has penetrated before,
And I don't,
No, if I bury it,
Or just move on,
But I do,
I look like I'm living,
And that's a secret,
That I do carry...
SLB

You go through the questioning of why did he die? Could I have done more? It is normal to question. Looking back I would say, just accept it. We are not on our own time. We are on God's time. If we can accept that we will know whatever happened, we could not have done more, he had to go with God. We must remain here. Whatever chose to help others or not is our free will. We also are on God's time, so we might as well be of service to Him.

Reaching out to the phone to call, running to the next room to tell him something, yes that is normal. Yes it kills you every time you realize over and over it is done. It is finished. You will only speak spiritually from now on. Somehow be grateful that you understand how precious a gift that truly is.

It's Not Fair

It's not fair,
    That tears fall upon my face,
Unable to breathe,
    To gasp,
It's not fair,
    That my burdens,
    Lie with only me,
When you,
    Should share them as well,
It's not fair,
    I have been but kind,
Not a single hurt given,
    To another,
    Yet, I weep,
It's not fair,
    My weeping remains,
    A constant,
    Please-I beg,
It's not fair,
    It's cruel,
Why, I cannot explain,
    Coughing, breathing, uneasy-
    Not being able to breathe,
I conclude,
It's not fair...
SLB

How did I get on with my daily life without crashing? Totally. Here is one idea I actually came up with myself a poster board. You get a great big poster board and put it in front of you when you are alone at home. Revise it every six months. Write down things to make you feel happy for a few minutes. Write down things such as exercise to keep you fit. Write down all your friends you wish to visit. Write down all the places that are close to go to that are fun. Write down the books you want to read and the movies you want to see. Then whenever depression starts to hit and it usually does. Look on your poster and go do something. Sometimes it might take you just an hour to do ten things it doesn't matter keep going. The next day do the same. I even wrote down exciting things to look forward to and special things I wanted to accomplish in six months. It's a mind game but it does work.

During the grief process many questions will go through your head. I had many and may I list some of them that it might help you see whatever you are thinking others have felt the same. I worried that he would be disappointed in me for not being able to handle his death. I thought he wanted me to grief faster and go on with my life. I told him in spirit form, that I would have always loved and cared for him and grateful he was in my life, no questions asked. I tried to console myself with going through these questions and answers I made up while thinking deeply over him. I thought about the aspect of that we both wanted a long and happy life. Could it have been prevented? And then it occurred to me to thank God for the time I had with him and not worry about the time I hadn't had. God knows best and I let it go. I wondered if he sees everything from Heaven and concluded that he does. This made me jubilant. He would be the one person other than my parents to help me with all my problems on Earth. He would watch over my children especially in times of war, which put great comfort on my soul. He would help mend all my relationships and protect us in bad weather or when potential harm might come to us. I was relieved He would be my companion in heaven if not on Earth. He would be there at the end of my life when I went to my heavenly home. I had talked to mediums and he had assured me he would watch over me and welcome me home when the time was correct. How would I know if he was with me? I was to speak his name or think of him three times and he would come to be at my side. If I was in meditation he would give me answers. He would never leave me. Trust that he is there and believe were the two words he gave to me. We live in each others' soul group and thus we would always be together through the ages and lifetimes crossing each others' paths. When we would be in Heaven all would be made clear before the next lifetime. After death the soul has the ability to be at more than one place at a time and therefore can come to us when needed. It is actually a simple concept much like Jesus or the archangels can be at many places at one time as needed after death we begin to have those abilities as well.

Grief may still pay you a visit when you least expect it. It can hit hard at holidays or sentimental places. I found deep prayer helps at those times, because it feels like a small depression could start to edge in. Remember you need to get through one day at a time. If going to church gives you comfort do it. If you need to keep busy and you are not working there are many activities at churches that are good to get involved with. Even today if I start to feel sad going to church refreshes my spiritual self and I am again able to concentrate on my life. I don't believe there is a time line for people. We can bring them up at any time and get a smile on our faces with remembrances.

Grief You Knock Upon My Back Door

Grief you knock upon my backdoor,
For on my front door I hid my grief from others,
It is not fair to listen to my thoughts,
Life and its happy thoughts should surround us,
But I hear the sound of a bird while in the park,
I hear the waves crashing along the coast, as I
    waddle in,
Reminders of a yesterday, that drew me back,
To a simple time, when grief had not yet left a mark,
I do not invite you to come, I dare not tell of my
    troubles,
So I go along each day, with silliness masking my heart,
Endlessly awaiting the day, grief will leave forever,
And only true happiness will knock thereafter,
On that door that faces my willows,
Where grief is never going to be welcome anymore...
SLB

God, Jesus, and the Holy Spirit is the only three in one that can put us back together when grief strikes. This is some of what I feel helps bring us a little closer to coming through the grief stage.

Read the Word of God daily, the Bible. Use the words that God spoke to comfort others who are grieving as well as yourself. Pray for the needs of others on a daily basis. I know the idea of loneliness and when we share what Christ taught us to do by helping others through loneliness; we are by that deed helping ourselves as well. I have known grief and by knowing grief I can help others with the pain of it. I can pray because I know the power and strength of prayer. I can see what love is capable of doing rather than the negative aspects of anger and hate. I can fully forgive and ask for nothing in common. And last I can fully understand the power of unconditional love.

During the grief process our emotions deplete our energy, and because of this we have no energy to change our lives or give ourselves to others. We are healing. We are sometimes angry and need to blame. The emotions of fear, anger, hate, sadness, envy and betrayal appear. In time you will see forgiveness is the only way to heal. Acceptance of what happened and where you are in life is what is needed. You will have forgiven the person for dying when you can say their name and it doesn't upset your daily life. This process shows you can also be taken anytime. Enjoy every moment and be happy will eventually become your standard message. Live in the present.

Grief...it is a stage of life that must be experienced at the time, to allow our new stage of life to appear...

SLB

Chapter 7
God's Help Through Prayer

God speaks to us...We need to Listen...

The power of prayer, it does heal.

Whether we do conventional prayer, or meditations allowing healing energies to go thru us it is important to stay close to God. In the metaphysical side of the Bible we see creation as falling from the consciousness of God. The serpent puts ideas into our mind. We are left with the need to fall back into the consciousness of God, which is called God consciousness. The soul body is at full consciousness with God being the first plane of consciousness after the great divide, between heaven and earth. When coming down for this life we remember life is only spirit, and how does soul appear. The individual being of Spirit is Soul. Spirit is used to create and that is life. That is our free will, when we come and have our individual lifetimes we are in search of God and finding our way to God, the one who created us. It is so simple yet so complex. Spirit is the heart of teachings, and only Spirit heals. Spirit can heal anything. Open your heart center with no fear.

As the lotus flower opening up with overwhelming love, meditation and prayer opens your heart center, takes away fear and fills it with love. Time and silence give us a chance to hear God speak. In silence we are soul. Your body needs to nourish the soul. Develop a relationship in silence. Try to be silent for twenty minutes. Your mind gets jealous of the silence. In doing that you get inside more of you. The purpose of meditation is to go deeper within yourself. You can go very deep to your ego. In silence you can see the part of you that is eternal. There is a great peace in that. This is your chance to be you. This also shows us life. Life is more than ourselves. We are all interconnected through each other and God. Meditation helps us understand life and our place in it through our deep connection with God. It is truly amazing. May God Bless...

Prayer is very powerful when you pray with someone in spirit who is helping you. Your prayer gives them strength and your love. They appreciate when we communicate with them and give them respect and honor by helping us.

Though You Are Not In My World I Feel You

Though you are not in my world I feel you,
I honor and give you your utmost respect,
For you have willingly come to my aid,
When all I did was reach out my mind to yours,
Help me to understand that you and I are of one
    with God,
When you desire to help me in my Earthly life,
I am also fulfilling your mission to help those who
    request,
Thank you as I look upwards to the heavens,
Please come and help me in my need,
I am indeed grateful for all you have done for me,
And when I too go from this existence to my true
    home,
May I continue to spread the blessings to those in need,
Continuing the ever lovely circle of prayer,
That God has entrusted before us...
SLB

Matthew 21: 22

And all things, whatsoever ye shall ask in prayer, believing, ye shall receive.

Jeremiah 1: 12

Then said the Lord unto me, Thou hast well seen: for I will hasten my word to perform it.

My Strength Lord

This takes strength Lord,
That I must renew through you,
Your holy water, your heartfelt songs,
Your Psalms of love,
Help my heart to heal, Heavenly Father,
Help me,
Stop this agony, I beg of you,
This hurt so deep,
How can I pull through?
Yet, Somehow,
Someway, I pull myself up,
Just for a moment, just for a moment,
My inner self speaks to me,
It is to God,
I must release my soul, my pain,
It is only to Him,
Can I dare to go forward?
So I beg, I plead, I pray, if not whole,
At least make me a part,
A small, yet whole part,
That through faith,
The pieces will come together again,
And only through,
The will of God,
I step forward, one step and then another,
With the hope,
I will not fall,
But go slowly forward,
With-the Will of God...
SLB

I Am Connected To God

I am connected to God,
Feel my presence in your life, so real,
I am connected to God, hold unto me,
As you pray and kneel...
Some have seen how we are as one,
You my brother, are starting this process,
As many you are God's son...
SLB

Dear Jesus,
Let the Laws of Nature be balanced,
Master my destiny Lord,
For the highest Will of God,
For all concerned...Amen.
SLB

Lord, As I Sit By The Sea,

Lord, as I sit by the sea,
Allowing it to forcefully put me at peace,
The sky and ocean are as one,
The hues of the pastel blues, not allowing a horizon,
As I stare upwards, my feet buried deep into the sand,
I remember your face Jesus,
As you shone the outline upon that sandy beach,
Is this now how we speak, my Father and I,
Peacefully hearing His voice cradled in the waves,
Whispering thoughts and causing my mind to wander,
I do believe it is,
So I'll walk Lord upon your shores, and listen,
Obeying your direction you set forth for my life,
And I will still look if the horizon still might appear,
As I stroll this highway, your perfect way,
Along this Carolina shore, I call home...
SLB

Our Dearest Lord,
May the good Lord always watch and keep you,
May He bless every person you care for,
Ever cared about,
Or will care about in the future,
And may everyone's blessings be fulfilled...
Amen.
SLB

God is Love, Love is God
I AM
I am a divine one from God,
Love will heal everything,
Thy will be done,
God, thy will be done,
For the greatest good of all,
Let it go, give it to God

Let God be your center. Put God above all else. God in His mercy will heal. You may not believe and it may take so long you wonder, why do I have to suffer Lord, do you not see what I go through daily. He does. It was our free will that was given to us enabling us so many experiences on this Earthly plan. May of us go through this and somehow we make it. I do not wish it on anyone but in our life's paths we must go through these hardships to see the perfection of the face of God. In truly focusing on God the Father you will pull through. I never lost my belief and though I asked the big question why, I did not argue. God is God, and I but a humble child of this universe.

God is always with me. His strength gives me hope. God is a miracle. The Incredible Miracle of knowing God. God is within all of us. The kingdom of God and our past lives live within us. Our body goes back to spirit when we die, our life is spirit manifested to experience life. Our souls go back to God, and we as individuals on Earth sometimes may need to lead others back. Feeling His presence and knowing whatever happens, God is in control. What a beautiful miracle to allow God fully in your life. To love Him with a pure heart and to do what is right according to Him. One is the miracle of a loving family. Life is full of small miracles, and I am grateful every day that I see and understand how beautiful life is. Thank-you God, for being my Savior. For helping me to understand your word, your way, and Lord always be by my side forever and one day.

Take Me My Lord And Into Your Arms May I Rest

Take me my Lord and into your arms may I rest,
For I am weary, I have been challenged by my tears,
My heart does not fully understand your will,
Yet, I give it to you to help me facilitate my being,
Looking toward your nature, I see your majesty,
Feeling your wind blowing against my face,
I know your strength and power take hold of me,
But my grief is so real, sometimes I don't know,
How do I go along?
It is then, I ask,
Take me my Lord and into your arms may I rest,
Hold me as your loving daughter, upon your chest,
Wipe away every tear that comes upon my face,
Give me unconditional love, to face my day,
You who knows the depth of my grief,
Fill my being with angelic peace for me to try,
And when I get weary, and I cannot go on again,
It is then I will ask you, and you I will depend,
Take me my Lord and into your arms may I rest...
SLB

Our prayers have strength. Talk to God all day if that is easier for you but pray. In prayer you are given your strength. Please always pray positive blessings toward others. All prayers and desires are heard. When we pray lights of truth go up to the heavens. When we pray for other people the prayers are truly heard. Parents always have a special bond with their children. The mothers' prayers that she has for her children are very strong. It is an amazing bond. It is very precious and a very special love. Your mother and grandmother will help you in many ways by asking them for their prayers as well. I ask mine as I still feel the love has not ended.

I have found the power of the worship service in addition to prayer helps tremendously in giving comfort in times of great grief. I would immense myself in the diversity of services all in accordance to showing worship to Our Father. The actual coming together with fellow believers and having kind gestures helped even if they did not know my grief. Volunteering at various church functions is also a way of serving the Lord, while helping yourself heal.

I do believe prayer unites the people of the world. There are prayer chains and such a blessing to all of us. When one or more pray together there is strength. If we as individuals ask our angels, archangels, guides, masters, saints and all those who love and care for us in heaven to pray with us we could be very calm and wise. Your friends may be half way around the world but you can pray for them. I do and when your grief is so hard you cannot bear it, praying for them or a stranger will actually lift your spiritual self into a giving attitude and that will promote healing as well.

Through Prayer Peace Is Obtained

Though prayer peace is obtained,
For as we sit quietly obedient to Our Maker,
Letting our thoughts and minds open to Him,
We let in the miraculous mysteries of the universe,
Unfolding into our hands as we pray,
Touching our solar plexus,
Feeling the energies flowing upwards, My thymus,
Pausing ever so quietly, still to the world left behind,
It is here we connect, we are with God,
We are one with God,
But when our energies focus on our innermost core,
We feel the pull, the need to be with God,
The absolute need,
That energizing yet all-knowing feeling of connection,
Will lead you back from where you did come from,
Your Source,
And that indeed will heal any hurt,
Grief-that stands between you and The Almighty
    Father,
And to Him alone shall we give all Glory...
SLB

As I Sit In Your Pew

As I sit in your pew Lord,
Concentrating not on my own, but of the rest,
For they have burdens Lord,
Perhaps much worse than I can confess,
Help me to see compassion in their eyes,
Whether in prayer or stillness,
Teach me to lay down my worries to you,
Helping those around me pray for their intentions,
Cleanse my heart of any wrong doing,
Heal my heart of its misery and grief,
That through your word I may see the needs of others,
And as I go to sit in my pew,
Feeling the majestic spirit that you alone can give,
Wishing for all their needs today Lord,
And leaving mine down for you alone to handle,
While I pray here in your pew,
Alone, on bended knees...
SLB

While praying to God keep your heart center open. It is important to have your heart chakra open to God while praying to Him, especially while you are in grief. Focus as much love in your heart and concentrate light and love to God while in meditation or prayer. The more love you give out to the world and God the more healing and the faster it will come. I am aware not to rush grief it takes time to work out, but this helps. Be patient with the process. When you have love to give you will receive love back.

I believe some of us were chosen by God because of our immense faith to teach others just by our presence, that feel of being around the person. I do feel that in fact I am honored to be in the presence of many of my friends and family who give me such peace. Through deep love toward God your aura will lighten the way for others. These people are the ones I believe God gives to us to help us through our grief, a gift of God.

You Who Have Such Faith,

Dedicated to my daughter Suzy, sons Paul, Robert, Mickey, and my first cousin Colin who showed me first hand his strong beautiful faith

You who have such faith, I do hope to somehow
    compare,
You show your Belief in the actions you project,
Others are inspired by just the way you lead your life,
Spreading the word of God through your mere
    presence,
People feel your aura of divine light and love,
Radiating downward from the hand of God,
Keep us all in your daily affirmations and prayers,
Hold those who have not found their way back to God,
By just leading your lives in such strong belief,
And when it is time for you to leave this earthly realm,
May the gates of heaven open wide with celebration,
Your embodied sense of all knowing, you were a gift
    from God,
And truly helped those on Earth, to Believe...
SLB

The Burden Of Silence

For you have not given me words,
For your words would have been of comfort,
I held on to your words, but they are memories,
My ears wanted silence to break,
But you were not with me,
You live in another time and place,
Break down the barriers that exist,
Lift up the doorway to heaven for a time,
Let me hear once more the sound,
That voice that could sooth my soul,
For it is the silence that puts grief in our hearts,
The heaviness that it carries,
The burden of silence...
SLB

To My Lord And Savior Jesus Christ Of Nazareth,

To you my Lord do I fall upon my knees,
To you only do I praise and give glory,
For you have saved me and those I love,
You have saved my ancestors, those who live with you,
Those who are a part of me, and of you,
I affirm you are my God, my Trinity, my Truth,
To you do I thank with all I have, and give Glory,
Whatever Your Will, it is, and shall be,
I affirm my acceptance of what is,
Thanking You precious Jesus for all that is,
Thanking You for all I have been given,
And not for what has been taken,
For it was done in Thy will,
May this be my prayer, My Lord,
In the name that is above all others Jesus Christ...
Amen.
SLB

To Find Oneness In God

To find oneness in God, and to feel total Love,
Truly heals the wounded heart,
God is our first, and we are to but follow,
Be active in our life, but not attached,
For if something is taken from you, you have God,
To know yourself, totally in one with God,
That is beautiful, and will fill your soul,
Through meditation to God,
Your senses find discipline,
And contentment in self,
Quiet yourself through reflective prayer,
Love the Godliness in you,
Such confidence will abound in you,
As you are one with God your Creator...
SLB

Lord Allow Me The Solitude

Lord,
Allow me the solitude, to hear your message,
In this quietness, there is understanding,
A peace that uplifts my soul,
Purifies my heart, as if giving it rest,
For my thoughts have been taken by You,
You who can handle all my anxiety, stress, dismay,
I am at total peace, that You alone can give,
So allow me to sit, quietly for hours, days, if I must,
Patience my virtue, shall I learn,
In this simple church of Prince of Peace,
I sit looking at the hymnal of St. Michael,
Where his mighty arms as a Guardian angel overlooks,
Keeping me safely in his vigil,
Allowing me my quiet, my calm, my life...
SLB

My God So Precious

My God so precious, You hold my life,
You who are all powerful, the great I AM,
Make me humble in your presence,
Command me to kneel before your throne,
As I but a mere spectacle of life, You touched,
Let me be forever grateful for all You have given me,
And as I hold my hands together,
And bow my head down to worship Your Grace,
May I remember how precious You are Lord,
So precious indeed, that you gave me life,
And now hold its majesty in your hand...
SLB

God...Let my prayers always be, my poems of love to you...
SLB

Chapter 8
After Life In Heaven

Let me tell you about the afterlife as I know it. There is love and peace, and they love us very much. All our loved ones are cheering us on.

Do You Hear Me?

Do you hear me as I look up into the heavens and pray?
Or do my tear soaked eyes speak words beyond,
What do I know?
I comprehend,
For they have taken you from me,
This universe,
The faith that you would not leave,
Yet, you do not remain,
I do,
Do you feel the same pain I do?
Do restless nights of longing,
Turn into days of wonder,
What truly happened?
Is this the worst nightmare, I must bare,
Or is this my new reality,
I did not ask for this burden,
Take it back, Lord,

Return his soul to mine,
For my heart cannot cope,
It knows not how,
Yes, do you see my face?
Unrecognizable to you,
You who have never seen such tears,
You who have not felt my grief,
Until you took your place,
In that heavenly home,
Will you call my name?
To be taken home,
Or must this torture remain,
Tears, a constant reminder,
Of you,
You who are not here to speak my name,
You who are not here to hold me,
Taking away grief,
Yet it remains so still,
Yet, I look into the distance of the night sky,
Knowing you are there,
Looking down upon me,
Feeling my grief,
Knowing full well my heart,
And if I to shall recover,
To one day,
Carry on...
SLB

I do believe in life after death, reincarnation, and the power of prayer. People have questioned me about my faith. How can you not be happy if you believe? Grief has a hold on you. Yes you understand, yes you love God, and yes if you are like myself you can still communicate with those in heaven. It is the closeness about the person taken from you while you are on earth, that you grief. You miss the person, the touch, the communication. It is difficult when you are aware that they are with you in a different dimension, yet we want them here the way that makes us comfortable. And until I went through every grief step I was not able to totally accept, even though I did believe in life after death in heaven. I knew that person was in a better place looking down upon me with peace. I do understand that the person in heaven can feel your grief, your anger, your deep hurt in their heart. They are on the other side of the veil. They too are learning what it is like for you and what they are experiencing. Heaven is glorious but their love for us remains. They watch over us while experiencing their own separation from us. Understand that that when we work through our grief we are also helping them move on to what they are doing in heaven. I was told through a medium he told me I am stifling him, because I will not let go of him. Every thought and anything I do is about him. Yes but that is normal after a death. I learned to slowly let go but you need time.

When I was thinking about heaven several questions came to mind. Did he while living a human life understand love? Did he understand that I sincerely, would rather have him living in any capacity than in heaven? What does he do in heaven? If I need him can I call upon him? Will he help me watch over those I love especially those that live under the perils of war and uncertainty? Will he be there when I cross over? Is there anything he wants me to do for him that he cannot do, because he is in heaven? Does he understand now that he lives in heaven I would have done anything I could to save his life? Can I just reach out and talk, and he will always hear? So many questions knowing that if I search my heart I truly will know the answers.

Heaven is real, and they are living beautiful lives there. I have had the honor to speak to many people on this journey about life after death. I have communicated with loved ones that have passed. It warms my heart with each of these experiences. They have stated facts that only that particular person and I would know. They have told me the sweetest of words and showed comfort beyond the grave. The veil is truly lifting as our ascension process gets closer.

Amazing That We

Amazing that we go between these veils,
   others do not see,
Amazing that we see beyond what others state,
   are normal existences,
Amazing that we both followed each other,
   your world and mine,
Amazing that we live beyond what we are taught,
   Rather provoking our inward thoughts,
Amazing that we see the pure artistry of your life,
   living both there and by my side,
Amazing that we can speak as quick as we wish,
   By calling out your name three times,
Amazing that we concentrate our thoughts,
   mastering mind to mind transfers,
Amazing that we with just the touch to our heart,
   feel the other through the veil,
Amazing that we share enlightenment,
   from soul to soul,
Amazing that we never separated you and I,
   with transcendental communication you never
   said bye...
SLB

Hold Me Close Just A Lit Bit

Hold me close just a little bit,
Let me manifest the glory of the other side,
For it is in knowing you,
I see,
I feel the presence of God,
Magnificent you say,
I can't imagine,
For we leave, as we come to this life,
The oneness with God,
Until we are reborn here again,
And as it imparts upon us,
Feels and unfolds in turn revealing,
The true splendor of God's kingdom,
You know, you are there,
My welcoming angel,
Upon whom I can always depend,
My way-
    Welcomed back,
As I too shall return,
So much more splendor,
So much more glory,
Be given to Him,
Who created us,
    As I fall now back asleep,
This to shall provide, such peace,
Endless peace with hope of wonder,
    Yet to come,
And faith instilled in me,
Of such awe,
I bow down humbly,
Crying in awe, of Our Lord,
Tenfold shall we know that Glory,
Hallelujah!!!
SLB

I Look Outside Fighting Back The Tears

Oh, I look outside, fighting back the tears, so deep,
   Waking up remembering, I reached for you, while
   in my sleep...
Some days the heart is hard to bear,
   Beauty surrounds me, yet I don't exist here, I just
   stare...
Even though many problems, I have to ponder,
   My mind doesn't concentrate, for you I wonder...
Wishing to be cradled in your arm,
   Knowing they are all, my world; and now will be
   safe from harm...
For you have a way of knowing my strive,
   Bringing hope, peace, joy and love to my life...
Longing deeply I crave you, oh the missing is so hard,
   Poetry flowing out of me, with love on your card...
Is it enough, I reach to hear your tender word,
   Messages of comfort and love, like before I've heard...
But oh how heavy the heart does appear,
   When sometimes my Sweetheart, my angelic force
   is not near...
Yet darling I'll be strong and put my hand to my heart,
   My darling I feel you, oh Sweetheart at last we are
   not apart...
SLB

Who Do I Turn Too?

Who do I turn too?
No one knows,
No one understands,
Why, I can ask myself all day,
But, it doesn't help,
I must go through this,
Come out, someway,
Now, I don't know if I can,
I wonder,
Restless, no sleep,
Contemplations,
Echoing my once quiet rest,
My head connected to another realm,
Where I want to remain,
But am told I have to return,
There is much peace there,
He and I together,
But this world,
This reality,
Which I deal with,
Is pain, torment?
Wandering endlessly,
Room to room,
Not knowing calmness,
And I go outside,
Look up to the universe and ask,
Peace,
Please Lord, give me peace,
I surrender,
To Your Will,
Only, Your Will...
SLB

We have the opportunity to see and speak to our loved ones after they have passed on to their after- life in our dreams. Have total faith and you will be reunited with them some day. If you experience a loved one talking to you, in your dreams, that is their way of communicating with us. Dreams are fascinating and much has been written on them. Try to write them down if they communicate in a dream, for not just comfort but so you do not forget what they wanted to communicate to you about. They usually have a message for you. They guide you and as I was missing them, I received a message of my life purpose. Be open to what messages come through in your dreams.

I just had my third New Year without him, as this third one passed I felt his presence so strong in the church we had attended, and this poem fell into place, as it should.

You Are With Me, This First Of The Year,

You are with me, this first of the year,
You touch my hair,
As I feel your presence,
Listening to Bach, in this church we sat together,
God has not taken you,
But allowed you to remain,
My constant companion,
In life and death,
You do not leave me,
As I sit,
Contemplating a new year, a new life,
You remain,
I understand how God shows us,
We are never divided,
We have our own paths to lead,
And you shall be my soul,
My love forever,
Neither distance, nor death,
Shall separate our souls,
For my love shall remain,
Just in a different avenue of thought...
SLB

Have we lived in lives with these people before? I do believe we have, reincarnated on Earth with those of our same soul group. I have had very well known mediums tell me about my previous lives with many in my family and friends. We have led past lives with many of our close connections on earth. There are many things we don't understand in our reality until we cross over. There is no jealousy in Heaven just unconditional love. It is unlike what we can imagine on Earth. We chose to come down on Earth at a particular time to learn something or work out a past karma. The soul in heaven earns the right to stay and not reincarnate. The reason you keep reincarnating is so that we learn everything we need to learn. After that our soul becomes a spirit guide to help others. Our soul remains with us through all our reincarnations. We need to understand our soul and its connection to God, and to feel this connection it is evident when we feel our spiritual connection through our heart. You can even meditate on these questions for answers. It is similar to a giant puzzle and our lives with all the small pieces fit together perfectly when we are finished.

You Surround Me With Your Thoughts

You surround mw with your thoughts,
Never finished,
As I put them down,
My hands quivering every touch,
Mind to mind we work,
Distance and spheres of existence,
Have been erased,
As if you have a chance,
A connection so clear,
To tell me your thoughts of life over there,
God is the Truth,
The capital T,
Believe,
As you whisper, I should have believed,
Your kind words fooled me,
Into not knowing the depth of your thoughts,
Your calmness, eluded your spiritual gift,
My doubts, I ask why I ever did,
Was the trial to much to handle?
I had to bare it,
Yet you had trials,
And they remain to this day,
I send my thoughts,
For you alone to decipher,
And quietly, at the end of the day,
Look up, where I do stay,
Knowing, my thoughts are as yours-
And-yours as mine...
SLB

Love Lives On

Love lives on, or so we are told,
I know I experienced it first hand,
I felt his presence,
Not of this world,
But of the next,
As if we had exchanged these thoughts,
While dwelling in this world,
And so I knew,
I was privileged to be of the few,
The ones that feel Earth and heaven,
Daring to be silent,
For others would talk,
Not understanding,
Years spent perfecting such a connection,
But reality proved me wrong,
His presence soothed me,
Gave me proof,
Full explanations that life doesn't end,
And Love lives on...
SLB

Give Me A Kiss From Your World To Mine

Give me a kiss from your world to mine,
Show me your thoughts and feelings still do shine,
Maybe just a whisper of my hair do wave,
Showing me signs of concern, you gave,
One kiss would surely give me some peace, dear,
For by feeling your thoughts, I now have no fear,
You have shown me after life is real,
By the sweetest touch when I fall asleep, I feel,
And I patiently wait for that sign you send,
How it does help my precious heart to mend,
So send me just one perfect kiss from above,
As I shall treasure it, such perfect enduring love...
SLB

Call From Heaven

Oh Lord, make it happen, let me speak to him,
I'll ask the questions,
I dare not know, these many thoughts of mine,
Of how our Heavenly Father lives,
Where the angels fly, I wonder so,
The Heavenly choir, can you hear,
Hallelujah chorus sung in surround sound,
Is it happening now?
Could this call from my loved one be real?
Is that how his voice sounds in Heaven?
If so please allow me some time to say,
I'll send all my love, hugs and more your way,
Please let me in faster,
Open up that Heavenly gate,
I need to speak face to face,
I love you so, please always remember,
And I still ponder the question you can't answer,
Why didn't you stay with me longer?
It's driving me insane,
I guess you had your work to do, as I too,
Too many questions always seem to remain,
I have only one more moment,
The call from above does say,
Then I'll wish you happiness, joy,
Until I meet you that sweet day...
SLB

387

You Are My True Angel,

You are my true angel; the Lord gave to me...
You will always watch over me, and guide me,
Your true caring has been magnified in the glory of
    heaven,
Such unconditional love which is rare on earth, exists
    there,
So I hold in my praying hands, gratitude,
That if you are not physically with me, spiritually
    you are,
That I do not see is still very part of my life,
Orchestrating plans for my life, for my highest good,
So as I sit quietly overlooking the willows by our lake,
And with great respect, I give you thanks,
For caring me in times of trouble,
And celebrating my times of joy and happiness,
For you my sweet angelic angel I feel,
You are my true angel...
SLB

Talking about the after-life in heaven can be of comfort. We are not living without them; for they can still function doing their jobs in heaven while watching over us. Jesus is able to be in many places at once, as I believe once your spirit is in heaven; you are able to be in at least two places at once. I communicated with my Father who is in heaven through a medium, and he stated to me when I asked what heaven was like; and he said, "You experienced heaven on earth with your love for Bill." That to me was very special and precious. Our loved ones watch over us as long as we need them. I was searching for ideas once and frustrated if I had done enough, and a medium I highly respected told me a message, "You my Sherri are to do the work that is needed to do on the Earthly plane, and because you understand I will be doing the work you need to be done on the spiritual plane with you. I will always be there with just the sound of your asking, I will respond." It sometimes takes just these simple but meaningful messages to set everything in place again. When our loved ones are in heaven and if they are inclined to do so they may channel information to us through the help of us on Earth. Thank you to all the mediums you are doing a great service to those of us in need. I want all of you to know you can communicate with your loved ones. They do hear you. Please be very respectful and kind to them. Ask them for help and guidance. Be grateful that they come to your assistance and say thank you. They want to help us so much it is up to us to reach out and ask for their assistance. One of the last mediums I spoke to said, he noticed you took off your bracelet. I had just taken it off that morning. I looked up and said yes, it had taken me through three deployments with my son and I had never taken it off until today. I went home and put it back on knowing he sees me and whatever I do supports and loves me.

What Clouds Are You Beneath?

What clouds are you beneath?
As your heart looks upwards toward the sky,
I look, but I am not sure,
The beauty of your essence imparts my judgments,
And I am not clear,
Yet, I truly know where you lie, how you feel,
Your every thought,
Confusion I give to you, as you ramble throughout
    your day,
You feel, I know,
When I am drawing closer to you, my energy,
And love, as you with your tear soaked eyes,
Look upwards and question,
It is I that cradled you last evening, in my loving arms,
And you will always know, my heart is near,
For as our hearts will never be truly parted,
I will look downward upon you now, and ask,
For only your loving ears to hear,
What clouds are you beneath?
SLB

I have gone through a series of questions in my life, yet always realizing heaven is completely a given, I do not question that. There may be times I ask myself are they always with us. My mind knows the answer is yes, and through my studies' I have come to the realization they enjoy watching us as we do while we are living our spiritual existence. Our loved ones in heaven have soul bodies. They have full consciousness in their soul bodies. Their bodies are not limited as ours. They have multi-dimensional bodies with no limitations. They are very happy as a spirit, and can usually travel places in a blink of a thought. We should be happy for them even though we would prefer to see them as we did while they had human bodies.

I Don't See You

I don't see you, I try,
I don't see you,
Yet I do see your spirit gliding by,
This veil uplifted as I sit quietly on my bed,
Feeling your soft touches, running through my hair,
Shadows of hazing-appearing,
Not in my imagination,
But glimpses of another world,
Here beside us-
Under that veil-
That too quiet place,
That if we dare part ourselves-
We may glimpse, hope,
And I gaze-
Remembering,
Stars found in perfect darkness in my home,
As if to say-
I am here,
I listen now, fully aware,
There is a connection,
And I listen, meditatively,
I am your comfort messages,
Signals to bizarre to ignore,
I feel your presence standing by me,
At the bottom edge of the bed,
You come,
You give,
Comfort to me,
You know,

But never let me give up hope,
I whisper, your name,
And you come,
For reunitement with our love,
Our past, and perhaps our future,
Yet, not in this world-the next,
I see those souls,
Not in my half awakened state,
But clearly-
As if messages need to be heard,
And I the messenger,
Was chosen,
Speak to me then,
I am here,
I listen now,
Just a confrontation,
You had been,
And oversee my life again,
And with this purest of love,
I go on knowing you are always there,
With a whisper of your name,
Known only by the chosen,
New aspects of my life,
Not fully awakened yet, quiet,
For a whisper, and that was it,
As I gave you in life,
So you now, give to me,
Though from another land, another sphere,
I feel,
I know,
I am blessed, and all will be fine...
SLB

Is That You Little Hummingbird At My Window

Is that you little hummingbird at my window,
Awakening me out of my sweet morning sleep,
Pecking endlessly at my window,
Unable to move unless I call his name,
Yes I believe it is you, who comes to visit me at dawn,
Coming back during the day to share some news,
You endlessly peck at my window,
Your spirit upon me, as I go about my day,
But those endless inside jokes you play, for I know,
It is you, who asks him to grab my attention,
At the times I call upon you to question,
You have given me proof,
It is you as my little hummingbird at my window...
SLB

I want to send messages of love to heaven. Of course you can do it at any time although if you do something special, it would be more meaningful to you. I would suggest candles, quite music, and contemplation.

I Love You My Darling So Very Much

I love you my darling so very much,
    Don't ever worry; we'll be out of touch...
Just close your eyes, I will come to you,
    Smiling laughing, shining like a star so true...
Magically you can ask, and I shall appear,
    Sending all sadness, just joy to you dear...
And feel the love in my poem, for truly you understand,
    It was written with my heart into my hand...
For you to embrace, love flushing throughout you,
    Until we are together; through and through...
SLB

My Living Angel

My living angel,
No one convinces me you are here,
I know,
It is your breath that sweeps through me at dawn,
When I am so low,
And there is no one to turn too,
It was your hand that led me to friends,
As friends became my family,
It was you, who orchestrated that in the heavens,
It was you, who held the dog at bay,
When his revengeful eyes turned to calm,
When I whispered your name,
You protect me, and empower me,
You want the best for me,
As we walk this life together,
You in the heavenly realms, and I right here,
But I do know, because I feel your presence,
And my thanks go toward you,
For all you have done and continue to do,
Bless you as well,
We walk our lives ever entwined, ever together,
In the veil which has little separation,
And my life enriched with the knowledge,
I go hand in hand,
Myself and my living angel...
SLB

I have been extremely fortunate to know spiritual mediums as I consider friends in this life time. He has sent me messages through dreams in which I actually talk to him which is very comforting and through meditation which I hear soft whispers and the third way is through a medium. One of the most comforting thoughts was he said, "I love you and I can never pay you back. You loved me and that was all you could do. I love you so much." Words are a great deal to those of us in grief. They give us comfort and usually they will tell you something that only you would know to confirm that they are coming through to talk to you.

Our dreams enable us to communicate while sleeping with our deceased loved ones in heaven. This is not an everyday occurrence. Some dreams are given to us so that we can learn a lesson they are sending us. You may write the dream down and meditate over it to understand what the message may be. Dreams are used for spiritual growth, as in when we ask before going to sleep that our angels may come and give us messages. Our soul also gives us messages in our dreams. While we are dreaming the conscious and the unconscious minds communicate with each other. Some believe if you are having a bad dream you may be off the direction of your purpose in life. Clear direction from your soul mind is achieved if you listen to your messages in your dreams. An example many people can understand is the dreams talked about in the Old Testament in the Bible. We have had fascination with dreams since biblical times. Remember to value your dreams and write them down. The characters in the dream are you. You are the author of your dreams. And when our loved ones come to see us, appreciate the visit and time we have with them.

Our loved ones in Heaven give us so much love. All we need to do is feel the love of God and send blessings up to heaven and feel their radiance and warmth flowing downwards upon us. They want our highest good for all of us. Knowing that, I feel him looking down upon me with so much happiness and joy to send me. I accept it with gratitude and much thanks and appreciation. When someone dear to us dies we must see the greater picture, and that being the case we have a life but so does other people and all are equal to God.. God can orchestrate what is the best for all concerned that is why we call it God's will especially when we pray and ask for the highest good for all concerned.

I have had small visitations in the form of seeing him for a couple of minutes. In my dreams I was able to have longer visitations waking up to a very satisfied visit. I am told we get what we are able to handle they definitely do not want to frighten us. When I have had discussions with many of my friends I have found people to be open and honest with me and have told me similar experiences. It is a source of comfort. He has given me much advice from heaven since his departure and one thing he said, Sherri be as innocent as a dove and wise as a serpent. As long as I try to take care of myself and I need just a little nudge he will be there to watch and guide me. He has become one of my guides in my life and I am so grateful to that. He also guides my daughter Suzy and she is wise beyond her years to life in the after world and how the veil is slowly lifting.

The grand healing of God in which our body leaves this earthly plain of existence and goes toward home is beautiful. Soul is beautiful. Love is enormous, it is breathtaking to feel the enormous love from God as it radiates in heaven. Our loved ones want us to feel that. When you pray ask for that love to surround you and ask it to surround those you love here as well. He asked me from heaven to show humanity how to love unconditionally. He said I loved him so much it is not fair not to show the world how to love with all your heart. Love unconditionally as a mother loves her children and you will be doubly blessed. He said I loved you so much, I gave you away. What beautiful thoughts and in front of every one of you I send him blessings, all the beautiful souls in heaven blessings, and much thanks and appreciation for all they do for us daily.

You Send Me Messages

You send me messages, for it is your birthday,
A painting arrived, and was entitled Angel Bay,
It was Santorini, an island I spent lifetimes upon,
It was as if you called from heaven,
My angel sending your angel a gift,
The name how appropriate, Angel Bay,
Where you reside waiting for me to catch up,
Looking at the darkest of blue waters,
Potted plants cascading down the steps to the bay,
It was our birthday celebration together,
From your world to mine,
And for me to realize, the veil is lifting,
And what we feel is coincidence,
Is our understanding of God's master plan...
SLB

My gentleman stated, "Faith is daring the Soul to go beyond what the eyes can see." In other words Faith is total belief in God. God is total love for all souls. If we could just live that practice there would be heaven on earth, but we as free will beings must wait for paradise until we cross over.

It been two and a half years and I think I am doing very well. The people that love us in heaven want us to live while we are on earth to honor them.

This is written from what his point of thought might be, looking back to a life not with us at this time.

Every Prayer You Sent

Every prayer you sent, I telepathically heard,
Clear as though you spoke my name out loud,
It was you, who sent prayers asking our Archangels to
      intervene,
You who taught me to ask our Spirit guides for help,
The Ascended Masters guided you along your journey,
The Saints awaited every day for your requests,
For you understood the power of the word,
You understood the humbleness of prayer,
For you knew the depths of my despair, more than I,
The Etheric plane so familiar to your being,
Reaching always up to the Great Divide,
Where Soul and human align as one,
You were comfortable where others did not seek,
You sent messages of hope, channeling them to me,
You taught me to quietly listen to the wind as we
      would walk,
For in its streams of quiet melodies, God speaks,
You showed me the ocean as you stood paying homage
      within,
And the fierce thunderstorms with undertones of
      God's voice,
You did not waiver, but rather revere in his firm tone,
I now thank you from my present home; I see all,
All that you in your quiet sweetness,
Masqueraded from many that had not reached that
      final step to Ascension,
You spoke in both deep knowledge, but also with
      kindness misunderstood,
So continue your service my Light worker of God,
Knowing deep within your heart, every message ever
      sent,
Was acknowledged and heard from the Great I AM...
SLB

To Honor You

I'm giving you something to honor you, as you are
    doing for me,
I'm living my life on Earth as you live in heaven,
Graciously remembering those that have gone
    before me,
For it is my ancestors who have made me as I am,
Reincarnating into myself,
Fully aware their lives might have been mine,
So to honor those that have gone before, I honor myself
    as well,
All souls playing a part of each others, journey for a
    purpose,
To be understood when it is unveiled for eternity,
So please with all respect I honor you,
For your great love of country, for which you served,
And because of your service, complications you bore,
We live in freedom for your sacrifice,
I live a life I will make everyone proud to know me,
In service my own way, finding joy,
Serving our Lord in word, inspiring others in Faith,
And with that spirit within my being,
Your spark that once filled this Earth will again shine,
For your love is not stagnant, but flows through me,
Channeling what needs to be yet done,
For the highest will of God,
To honor you, as well...
SLB

It is approaching three years and I still receive messages...

The Blue Moon

Messages received on the morn of the Blue Moon,
It is you, as I remembered before,
For they played our song, "Let me be your hero",
And I danced not in your arms, I remember,
But in those of a dear friend who understood,
And just as it comes upon the third anniversary of
    your passing,
You send thoughts, a connection I can feel,
"You were always on my mind",
As you were with me,
Choosing Elvis, my favorite, to sing this melody,
And giving us a connection between our worlds,
For love does not extinguish,
You have taught me to believe,
Your appreciation during your life,
I do know, and understand your need to do more,
For in your world you do more than could have been
    done here,
You are my angel,
As I am to be an angel in writing to others who mourn,
And so I do, not daily,
But through inspirations of St. Theresa, perhaps my
    guides, and especially you,
For you have my best interest always,
I shall carry on,
As your angel on earth,
As you my angelic force that never leaves my side, in
    troubles,
And rejoices with me, in happiness...
SLB

A rose petal lies upon my bed post,
as I lay down to sleep...
SLB

Chapter 9
Recovering By Learning To Live Again And Memorials To Our Loved Ones

Make life about something more than myself...

The experience of hospice whether going through it as a caregiver or patient is a very difficult task. Would I ever want to do it again? No. Would I do it again? Absolutely, love has a way of healing us making us stronger and able to cope with what life hands us. I am a better person for have gone through hospice. I love the Lord, I will forever in my heart say God is great, God is gracious. And to the gentleman who taught me more than I can write I would like to say, as Elvis wrote, "you were always on my mind."

The test of hospice gives spiritual growth. When it is all over your mind clarifies things in the correct balance, it might take time, but it will come, you will learn to accept and know you passed the test the Lord gave to you, be proud.

In order to have a higher spiritual growth certain difficult decisions have been written into our lives. People are introduced into a circle of friends to help with those challenges. Understanding this and knowing we most live through these learning sessions, enables us to trust God, knowing He wrote that into our lives. God does not judge us. We are our biggest critics of our self. We need to love ourselves as the perfect people we are. When we are faced with such life or death problems it challenges our spirituality to have a deeper understanding of God. How we fit into the scenario. God only gives us what we can handle, sometimes it seems too much, but we can do it.

Time Has Passed

They tell me, time has passed,
You are over the death,
Death is not something you are over,
It is something you live with,
Everyday, every hour,
You adjust,
Adjust your sails,
As your sailor truly did,
They too miss us,
As we miss them...
SLB

Beautiful Seashell

Beautiful seashell from the sea,
   Capture my heart, become a part of me...
For as I walked barefoot, and gazed down on the sand,
   It was you who captivated me, and said, take me in
   your precious hand...
The warmth of the hot sun radiates down from the sky,
   Bringing such ultimate peace and tranquility to my
   naked eye...
Castaway in this ocean this grief I thus have had to
   carry,
   Let my life from today on give me joy, and make me
   merry...
SLB

I dedicated my first half marathon to the one who watches over me...

Angel That Watches Over Me

My sweet angel that watches over me,
Thank you my darling for carrying me,
   In my half marathon,
You are the sweetest darling of all time,
You know it meant the world to me,
But for you to carry me,
   At times,
Allowing my body, rest,
Allowing me to do other tasks with angels,
Wow, amazing,
The power of angels...
SLB

I started keeping a journal of my feelings five days after the death. I now looking back on it see the progress. The first entry was about helping others. I wanted to make other people's lives easier by me doing tasks for them to allow them time to study. Every one of us is here for a reason at certain times and I believe I had least had a purpose. I knew I had the ability still to pray for other peoples needs so I wrote that down, and I knew I could make them dinner when asked. I had no idea how to do these simple tasks if I suddenly was hit by an enormous amount of sorrow or tears, but I would try. I wrote, "I will start to heal my aching heart, I need quiet, lots of quiet, healing foods for nourishment, solitude, friends and time for both. I feel so sad, I ate to nourish myself, and smelled the roses from the funeral."

I kept myself as busy as I could. I would go to work just to be able to socialize with other people. I wore makeup, dressed up and went out to dinner with family. I wrote," nothing helps and nothing ever will, but I have to try". My man donated his body to science and his eyes also, but not his heart. It was written in his health care power that Sherri has my heart, you can have the rest for science. One week after his death it occurred to me someone has his eyes. Someone in this world whom I might run across has his eyes. He wanted to help others and I believe he is smiling from heaven knowing the good he did.

His Eyes Still See

His eyes still see,
Not in his body, nor person, but through another,
Someone given a gift,
Too priceless to say,
Sight---
Given to someone after death,
The one whose eyes lit up when I came through the door,
One whose twinkle meant only for me,
And blue as the Aegean Sea, where we met,
Those eyes were mine,
Yet now belong to another,
His donation gave sight to one in need,
I will never know,
Whose eyes might look upon me,
Knowing it is I, the very one,
If they could speak,
After they see my smile,
Glancing through the crowd,
I whisper,
His eyes still see
SLB

Eight days after the death as busy as others were making me I noticed I was not dealing with the death. I tried to talk with others, text, email, write everything the books had told me to do, but I did not get relief. As soon as I was by myself I hit bottom. I would cry endlessly touching his picture asking questions, had I done enough, why did this happen to me, did I need more prayers, I turned into a confusion of concern. I wrote," I'm in a whirlwind, exhausted, trying to take care of myself, but so far I'm not doing well. I need to re-focus." I was given two extra large family concerns that others would have said one of these three should be enough, but God was indeed testing me. Why? Good question, perhaps so I did not have time to totally focus on my sadness. My loss was draining me as these other problems needed to be solved.

Nine days after the death, the questions started to haunt me. I wrote, "I have not had quiet." How does one recover when quiet is not allowed. I kept myself so busy, but I was totally exhausted from lack of sleep. I would cry all night and wander around when I was not at the active part of the day. I began to realize I had not done my Bible verses since his death and at the band concert when they played," Lady Ga-Ga", I began to cry. I was a living disaster. I was trying to hide it from my family, but actually having the word, "Sad" written on my forehead.

Ten days later you suddenly realize I can't call him. Turning around grabbing the phone throwing it across the room, has reality set in, did I finally get it. Oh my God screaming, what do I do. Had I been so busy trying, that I had put the simple ideas of I can not speak to this person anymore away from my mind. It is horrible beyond belief. The one you love taken and now I realize communication is shut down. At church that morning I do believe he sent me messages through the church program. Psalm 139 and James were both recited and I looked up and said thank-you you are with me and I need to see you differently. Does that help a small amount, believe me grief does not end there. It is your enemy not your friend. It comes when no other is around and haunts you. One just has to get through and it is not easy.

You're Still With Me, My Love,

You're still with me, my love,
    I feel the quiver, intensifying deep, inside my soul,
As you only can connect with me totally,
I look, I feel, I touch,
Yes, my heart looks, yet feels your presence,
    You have not left me,
You are everywhere I look,
Everything I touch,
The sense, the smell that envelopes me,
It is you,
I close my eyes, you appear,
    As no one else, does the same,
I exist, for the time we shall be together again,
    And whole we shall be,
    When I go home,
    And our hearts be united,
As they shall...
SLB

Eleven days into this I had stated such complete sadness, like I have never known. I worked all day to try and bury the pain, and when I got home I wanted to rest. I was not allowed that luxury my children occupied my time. Even talking on the phone is not therapeutic, my body was screaming rest, and until evening I was not allowed, my family and phone calls put a quite situation untouchable. He came with a penny on my car seat, and also did something out of this world, he took my little stuffed animal out of my pillowcase and put him on my bed. I checked with everyone it was him giving me a message from the afterlife, he was with me the best that it could, and that should be a blessing. The worst thing that people told me at this time was you will have a new beginning. Do not say that to anyone eleven days after a death. It is raw. I was happy with my life and now I have such sadness you cannot imagine. No it is too soon and I could not even imagine why someone could say that to me. Didn't they really understand the severity of the situation. My life would begin again, but not until this horrible pain went away and I wanted to let go of it.

I remember at night getting his pajamas out of my dresser and laying them on the bed beside me. I believe many people do that for comfort. One morning I woke up with them wrapped all over me, and with both a tear and a smile somehow I knew he would be there.

Sometimes you just want to cry. I wanted people to just let me cry. I will not punch anything but tears were a constant they flowed non-stop. I spoke to God asking how does one cope with this? I certainly don't know how. I wanted to cry all day and not worry about a thing. That is not my life but in my mind I thought it would be the ideal situation. I am totally beside myself because those closest to me except my daughter really don't want me talking about it over and over. I am supposed to accept it. Well I can't. Its too soon. I love him, I always will, so isn't there something wrong with this, he is gone. His words float through my head constantly we had a future, a long one, and it was taken from me. I have to rebuild but I do not want a future without him. I don't know how to be alright. I play useless solitaire just to get to another day. I just want him here with me. I didn't break up, I thought we would always be together, but death separates us. It is cruel. Tears flow too easy, and I don't know how to stop them. It takes too much concentration not to cry. I lie to others so they don't tell me to shut up. I lie to get through the day telling people I am fine. I know he is with me, I feel it, but I still miss him. Terribly, the way we were. You took away my best friend, the one person who knew every thought in my head. The one I could call anytime. This hurt doesn't stop. There is no way to explain it. And who really cares. I have to learn to live a life void of him. Knowing he wanted to be with me always. We thought we had all the time, but we didn't. it is not easy for him to see me suffer. He can't tell me how he feels. I need to be sympathetic to his feelings as well. He protected me so I need to let him go if I am able too.

I'm going into the twelfth and thirteenth days, my writing helps me. I am at work and it doesn't help. Nothing can solve the situation unless he is living. I can't call and I can't talk to him the worst feeling in the world. My heart is so sad, although I am aware I do want to work through this I don't know how. I suddenly see something I want everyone to be happy before I will allow myself to be. I realized I felt this way, because my heart is not ready to heal. I need to mourn the fact that he died. He is not here. I miss him, and I want to cry. Even if it is constant crying I want to do that. He cries with me from heaven and he understands exactly how I feel. I ended up calling friends and making plans for the weekend. Could I possibly eat, carry on a conversation, I was going to try. No one should have to go through this. Then it occurred to me try the over polite method never use harsh words to people, open doors, help people. Would that help? It masked the problem of my loneliness of the simple fact he was not here. I stare constantly at his picture hoping that will help. I listen to my voicemail at his voice and I still have the fading scent of the flowers he told me never to throw away.

Two weeks have passed since his death. I am experiencing devastation beyond, what should I do. I miss calling him and I miss telling him everything. He knows exactly what I do all day but I do not know what heaven is exactly like. I studied much on the subject, but this is raw, I am in so much pain I can't think about heaven yet. Everywhere I go I think I see signs that he is trying to communicate with me. I think I put him on a pedestal of never doing anything wrong. We as humans always do but when your loved one crosses over you imagine how perfect they were and forget the flaws. It is like they are in a perfect area that they never did any wrong.

The fifteenth day I told him heaven is beautiful and I hope he is happy. I told him I know I have to remain to do much needed work and help those who depend on me. It was a Sunday and I went to my church, my rock the church I was baptized and confirmed in the one that held me together when I felt my world had crumbled beneath me. People were telling me, you will go on. Guess what I don't want too, its' too soon. He is still my man. I am grieving the loss of him. Let me be, please let me be. Leave me alone. Please I need time. I need to heal. Is that too much to ask? I don't think so. Yet kind hearted people keep talking to me and I just want to be able to still hold him, talk to him, and not accept the fact he's dead. I am in grief. The pain in my heart is too much. I come into my home and while no one is there I scream. I scream as loud as I can I am in pain, I can't take this anymore I want to see his face, I can't talk to anyone, and I cry with such tears I never thought they would end.

The very next day the sixteenth day after his death, I had to hold my daughter up. Tragedy struck when her dear friend died at age 23. Suddenly the mother in you reacts my child was in pain, and yes I would do the best I could to be her rock. My perspective changed when my dearest daughter was shattered twice. She was basically caring for me and now this. I couldn't let her see my pain, I was her mother and she needed me. God puts many obstacles in our life but I would never wish that tragedy on anyone. She was but a child and left her dear sisters and parents, many friends and family and my heart broke for all of them. As it should I remembered it is to help people we are here and I better remember that lesson soon.

The seventeenth day yes I was in pain but I was going to learn to put it someplace and do what needs to be done. The following day we attended her funeral and yes it was my daughter I cried for and the beautiful soul we lost.

Continuing on with my grief the days that followed I still felt like a zombie, but I tried to hide it from my family. I watched movies, tried to smile, but deep down the awful truth was I was beyond sad but somehow I would pull through. Would it be work or perhaps studying, I guess I would try just about anything at this point. My mind kept saying how perfect he was, but in reality no one is. Grief tells us things to keep us at bay.

My sadness is getting unbearable and I need to somehow pick myself up from the bottom where I do believe my existence is at this particular time in my life. I had one cousin say, which made me very happy you always have me. Yes I am alive and I still have my family. I just need to process all of this and I don't know how long it will take me.

I started on all the websites on the computer to connect with him in the afterlife. I was devastated beyond what I envisioned. I found hope that he knows my pain and what I am dealing with, but he as well needs to move on and I am keeping him stagnant.

Shortly before his first month anniversary of his death I was still feeling no one understood my grief. I came to the conclusion which I should have always known, God cares. God must have had a reason for all of this. I do wish that people would not tell me he's better off in heaven and I am better off, that hurts. When you are in the state of taking care of someone you love, you don't mind. You would do anything for them out of love. That talk to me didn't matter, he is not coming back. Could I have done something better? It doesn't matter because he is not coming back. I need to thank God for allowing me to have the experience as long as I did. He didn't leave me, God took him to a beautiful place. Think of your loved one in that sweet angelic home where we all will be together some day.

It is the day before his first month anniversary of his death. I do believe my emotions go up and down to acceptance and denial. I wanted to go through the steps of grief quickly but my body is telling me otherwise. I'm lying and hiding the truth inside, I am devastated. I am not alright. I am in so much pain I want to scream all day. Oh my God my mind goes through the scenario over and over how he died and I want to replay it and change the ending. Why I cry out to God. I am totally afraid now if one month comes I can't go back in time and change this, the outcome. My reality knows I can't but my heart wants desperately too. Remember when everything was happy, I want that. Then I end up going places and finding others with stories more tragic than mine. I need to appreciate and be grateful, but this is one of the hardest things I have ever gone through and it doesn't stop.

Today is the one month anniversary of his death and I honestly can say it has been the worst month of my life. I kept myself busy with errands but my sadness is overwhelming. As soon as I have nothing to do even for a short time I cry. I have cried so many tears I don't know where they all came from. I have cried to me what seems like an ocean of tears, my grief is enormous. When I'm crying I want him to come to me and hug me stop all of this pain, but it never stops. I wonder if people know such grief and if they did, how did they cope with it? I never want this pain again and I never want anyone else to have to deal with it. I found on the computer a site for grief and then I wonder why I don't spend my time doing something useful and I come to the conclusion I can't, I go over and over in my head the same scenario until it is killing me. I do believe I am in deep depression. I scream out loud, why aren't you here, if you were I wouldn't be depressed and life could go on. Why did you leave me? I still have your flowers and I am so sad. I still have the flowers you gave me on the morning you died; the trinity of gardenias, the four roses you gave to me not knowing it was to be my final bouquet.

The Last Bouquet

You gave me roses, as my name was derived from the
  first perfect one,
You gave gardenias' in the power of three, the trinity,
You probably knew these would be my hope this first
  month,
Slowly they all faded, as I carefully kept the petals
  beside me,
They accompanied me as I drove that day to the
  church,
As I sat motionless at your service, unaware what had
  transgressed,
They accompanied me home, to later sit beside me as
  tears flowed,
I would later realize how precious a gift they were,
They remained with me that whole first month,
The scent lingering as the morning you gave them
  to me,
I could see your eyes so happy how pleased I was,
Your love had carried me this month through God's
  gift of flowers,
The very ones that meant so much to you,
Four roses, two white for the purity of God, and two of
  our favorite color,
As you said the three gardenias, represent the trinity
  for you...
SLB

The following month became a blur, much the same as the last. I tried to keep very busy to pass the time. I ended up working twelve hour days and I was literally so tired at night I would fall asleep. It was therapy for me. I took off work for one week six weeks after his death and went to the Edgar Cayce institute in Virginia Beach to get comfort. It truly helped me communicate with him at a higher level through concentrated meditation and much needed spa treatments for complete relaxation. I miss him terribly but I am going through the process and working through my pain. I had my birthday in Virginia Beach along with my best friend and together we put some of his ashes in the ocean, released balloons, and prayed. Later in the evening I saw him in the mirror and I knew life would eventually be alright. He had come to me on my birthday and I told him I love you, as he also said to me.

It was a good journey for me to go to Virginia Beach it had awakened what I always knew He was with me at all times. His physical body was gone but his spiritual one could help me in many ways. My broken heart in my earthly body had needed time, rest, and then it would remember what it had always known, life remains just in another form.

The healing that I so wanted would come from within myself I just had to ask and it would be done. God's healing power would be God's love for us.

Start To Heal Me Lord

Start to heal me Lord, show me how to look within,
Walk beside me as I walk the labyrinth,
Showing me quiet meditation will soothe me,
Teach me as you taught the Masters to go inward,
Loving caressing my life force deep inside,
Breathe the life force into me when sadness hardens
    my heart,
Help me remember all Souls' have a purpose to be here,
Equally heal my mind, spirit, and body,
Teaching me that healing comes from within,
Hear my mantras as I chant a song of love to you,
While raising my vibrational field to heal,
And as I do this Lord, let me never forget my loss,
Instead let me learn to live and,
Start to heal me Lord...
SLB

Two months after his death I went to his military funeral. It was one of the hardest things I have ever done in my life. I stood there after everyone left searching what was left of my dear Marine,

What Remains Of You Now

What remains of you now, as the military service put
    you to rest,
I stand watching your grave, with tear soaked eyes,
Looking upwards to the heavens, why am I still here?
A simple marker fills the spot where soon a cross will be,
So I fall upon my knees, my hands touching white roses,
The dirt still freshly put upon you beneath my body,
I cannot feel, I cannot move,
I am in a state of restlessness,
Sadness escalated with the reminders of my dear
    Sergeant,
In God's arms not mine,
And as I look to the left and right, white crosses in
    symmetry,
I know he is home, both here and with His Maker,
The Lord and Savior of us all, who created us from dust,
You are to be returned as you came,
And someday I too will be as dust with you...
SLB

The military service took a strong setback as emotions poured forth. I found comfort in dear friends I had met along the way. Even small conversations helped as I was now more accepting of condolences. I was carrying on and I knew he was very proud of me. He knew my broken heart was reaching out to heal, and with God's strong presence in my life it would. I had setbacks such as crying out I am in pain, but I believe time will heal. This pain you are not prepared for, it hits very hard and strong. It attacks your insides and fills you with hopelessness. I was not prepared, some say I should have been, and to that I respond, whoever is.

My Heart And Soul Live In Heaven Now

My heart and my soul live in heaven now,
God has provided you with a new home,
You are no longer at my home, but by my side,
You look down upon me as I see the red cardinal fly,
Tender thoughts fill me as I see a Panda bear,
For I know when you are reaching out to send me a
    word,
I do not fear when the angels will come one day,
For you shall wait for me as I finally return,
Greeting me as I enter into rest,
My heart and Soul finally at peace...
SLB

About nine weeks after his death I heard a simple message from him: "You can help me, so much more if you just accept it. I am in a better place, where there is no pain, you can help all of us, and I will be with you all the time in your heart, where Jesus lives."

I dreamed that I should not doubt the presence of my man, just trust, no matter what, he is there. He helps me with everything, and does not want me to be sad. That I should know he is there and always will be. He resides in my heart and can feel my heart whether it be happy or sad. When I choose to be happy he is also. When I feel sad or depressed he feels that as well. He told me there is nothing more I could have done. It was his time to leave. He tried very hard to stay, but it was his time. He was needed to do bigger and better things. He is able to watch over me in a better way in the third dimension. He understands my sadness and wants me to think at a higher ability and do good for others. He wants me to stop thinking I or anyone else can interfere with God's plan. Let him shine from within me by being a testament of Living Love...

It was the first holiday season after his death, three months prior that I attended a memorial service to those that had died during the year. It was called Blue Christmas at Grace Church. It was a service of remembrance and hope. There was a lighting ceremony of four candles, one each for grief, courage, memories and love. Each of us received a candle with the person's name on it. The candle also said, "When a loved one becomes a memory, the memory becomes a treasure." It also said, "Although death has separated us physically, faith and love has bound us eternally. We carry the light of your love, today and always!"

The first holiday season I believe I kept myself so busy and distracted to ward off the hurt. But it was painful. Everyone was concerned about Christmas and all I could think of was why was he gone? The greatest happiness I have ever known and it is not here. I miss him and love him dearly and I must have Christmas alone, not alone with my family, but without him. Sometimes I feel I exist in a shell, while he was alive I still had hope. It is gone and every day I will myself to get better. My son bought me a Pandora bracelet with symbols for both of us and it truly represents our love. While wearing it I feel the beautiful memories that we had. Merry Christmas Jesus he is in heaven with you.

God hears what is not spoken and understands what is not explained. For His love doesn't work in the lips, or in the mind, but in the heart.

Sitting in church I started to feel more compassion to those around me than to my own problems. Everyone has hardships to handle whether they are big or small. There is an old expression that God only gives you what you can handle. There are days I want to surrender to His Will and not even think anymore, but then I look around and know perhaps these people of the world need prayers and compassion as well. As we give to others whether in prayer or compassion, we are rewarded as well.

Look Around At God's People

Look around at God's people,
For they as I am, are the face of God,
Each as special as you and I to the One who Created us,
I feel,
I feel that their hearts are burdened as mine,
As they lay down their concerns at the Cross,
Awaiting an answer, we might not hear in our time,
For the One who knows all,
Does not always answer in the time we ask of,
God's time is unique, known only to Him,
And the acceptance of that, is Wisdom,
So I do feel,
For the flock of your fields,
The ones who have come for Your understanding,
Your healing of all troubles,
As I sit with hands praying up only to Your eyes,
Giving my concerns a rest this day,
Taking on the concerns of my brothers and sisters in
       Christ,
To focus my eyes in their names,
To be sympathetic to the needs of all others,
To fully understand the troubles of them are as mine,
For we are One with God,
What is mine is my brothers, and what is his is mine,
Lord, I do ask that their problems be settled,
And mine I patiently await for yet one more day...
Amen.

Their Sorrows

I know not their sorrows Lord,
As I sit quietly at prayer beside your cross,
Their sorrows may be deeper than mine,
They may have been tested more than I could bare,
I struggle Lord, put me obedient to your will,
For I only know what lies in my heart, not theirs,
Help me today Lord to put their needs before mine,
Every face I see may I bless with all I have,
Let my worries be not mine, but for them,
Let my time spent in prayer be cast for the needs of
    others,
As my life be put on hold,
Yes, Lord today awaken me to see their sorrows,
For your people are here with me,
They kneel before you along side of me,
They partake of your communion bread,
Let them forever be at your mercy,
Let the Blessed Virgin Mary hold them in her arms,
Just for today let me forget my needs,
As I remember the needs of my friends gathered here,
And as I do let me hold their sorrows Lord for them,
Let me cry their tears so they receive rest,
And let me sit Lord quietly in reverence to only You...
SLB

We Are As One

We are as one,
    You say,
Those of us who were lost,
Suffered beyond,
What most of us suffer,
Until a far older age,
The Lord gives,
    And the Lord takes,
The taking at times,
    Crushed us,
Into an unknown,
Vacuum of nothingness,
Our heart shattered,
    Beyond what could be-pieced together,
We don't try to explain,
There is none,
Nothing,
Just this burden,
    Agony,
Unreal feeling of total hopelessness,
My faith,
    Tested,
    Yes,
But the full reality of life,
    Without,
The stripping of one's soul-
Over and over,
Until there is no feeling left,
So surreal,
So unkind,
So unjust...
SLB

People live go on a journey for a while, and then you go on a journey with another spiritual partner.

Love lives on, I walked, I healed, and I did love again...

I Found A New Love

I found a new love, someone to give me a chance at
 living,
Someone perfect in my eyes, as I was in his,
So we danced a lover's serenade, of romance so grand,
Filling my soul with purpose, and a chance to be,
God has our master plan in the palm of His hand,
We are but the actors portraying our script,
As I felt the grief overturned with this surge of love,
I looked into the eyes of my new man, and knew,
He was mine, as I was his,
Suddenly, God gave me a gift to go forward,
It was as simple as can be,
It was love,
I found a new love...
SLB

How do you go on and build a new life. I did very slowly. I as well as many of you attended grief class. I went to three different ones. I attended these at the same time. The first was very structured with a book, movies, people who were there to try and help through the process. What did I feel? I felt numb and that my pain was so real how could I possibly listen or help anyone else. Grief is so strong. It is like a force controls you and all the polite words that are supposed to flow do, but you can't function like you would like to. You get up get coffee have a pastry, smile all the while wondering if this is helping, what is wrong with me. Yes the people were great it is just so difficult, time is what will eventually lesson the pain. The first one I attended at a church, it was called Grief Recovery support group. Pastor Graham had suggested that I attend and I am grateful that I did. It was run by Pastor Samuel T. Rorer and volunteers who had already taken the course. The church accepts anyone in the community that is in need of grief therapy. It had thirteen video seminars all dealing with the grief process. You could join the class at any time. Every video session was independent of the other. The second one was a one on one arranged by hospice. You are entitled to have grief counseling for up to one year after your loved ones has died in the hospice group. I had a private counselor. She asked me to write down my thoughts which I was already doing. She asked me to talk about my previous life and how I would go on. Did it help? I know she tried to help and that is all I could ask as with the other, time is what I needed. I did appreciate that the hospice group attempted to help me. The third group was also in a church setting. It was more of a social setting, in which we sat and talked about our feelings. Each of us talked about our individual loss. I know everyone did their best to help me. It is similar to other groups where you have people in common. It was so raw for me I could not feel myself even with people in common with me. I was so heartbroken I really never thought my life would ever feel normal again.

It was a time about nine months later after his death, after the worst possible torture I could bear that I found someone to love. I wasn't looking I was unaware that God could give me such a gift. Life would have a renewal I was suddenly needed in not just my children's life but in another. I was so grateful to the love that God gave me with this new man. I understood I could go on with my life and find a new purpose, and it was perfect. I was happy, content and completely satisfied that someone understood me so well and wanted the best for me as I did for him. I did not believe while I was going through the grief process I could feel, love someone so deeply again, but it is possible.

And when I symbolically took my ring off out of respect for the new man in my life I knew I was healed. I got through the most painful time in my life. With God my Father in Heaven, Jesus Christ my Savior whom I am eternally grateful for His sacrifice to us, and The Holy Spirit whom I asked constantly to flood me with grace and peace I had been blessed with a new awakening, a new birth and what I call a new life. I made it through and have so much love to give.

Our loved ones in Heaven do not leave us, they help us through our challenges in life. If we look closely we see signs that they check in on us and encourage us. I look for signs and yes I see them, it gives me great comfort knowing I am not alone in my journey here on Earth, but rather accompanied by those who have gone before me, and hopefully I will support those I love after I am gone. There are obvious signs and others not as noticeable unless you are looking. Some of the signs are pennies from Heaven, scents in a room (perhaps a familiar scent), numbers (that perhaps have a significant meaning), songs (sung that had a special meaning), dreams, etc.

While yes I did my best to live again. Some days were extremely hard and you did not know how to carry on, and some were easier. The following poems express a time when it took strength to live again...

Come Carry My Soul

Come carry my soul,
Through endless days of wonderment,
For I am left here on Earth without you,
Challenge my soul,
But allow me the luxury of knowing,
You are there,
You who sat next to me, your hand upon my thigh,
You whose eyes captured mine, even across the sky,
And when you did whisper,
It was your words I put to memory,
Sustain me in thought,
As I go about each day,
Measure all my tomorrows, as if you had stayed,
Nourish me, as only you can,
Allow me to be adventurous,
Wicked, some do say,
Allow my life to happen, my way,
But sweetness,
Look down upon me from all the heavens above,
Carry me on your wings of our love...
SLB

Can You Answer The Questions Of The Universe

God, if I sit quietly, can you answer the questions of the
   universe,
Or do I just accept, and remain still,
Why do some of us, have death our next companion,
When life seemed to just flow,
Is it karma to be re-paid?
Debts owed to this universe, we call home,
Or a strike of luck, run out,
Somewhere along the way,
I ask for answers,
Have you given me some?
You, the I AM,
Is this the cosmic plan?
Did I sign up for all this?
Can I change my mind?
Or do I have to live it out,
My mouth not uttering a word,
If I knew all the answers,
Would it ever change my fate?
Would it make me a true believer?
Would I perhaps understand; your plan?
Whisper me the answers,
As I sit Father, upon your lap,
Sitting here as I enter heaven,
Thank you Father,
For I know now at last...
SLB

You Freed My Soul

How can this soul-give thanks,
Try as I do, as blessed as you shall be,
You freed my soul-from pain beyond imagination,
The depths unexplainable,
For grief knows, how to live in a heart,
With manly ways and gentle touches,
You freed me, as no other,
Connections realized, as though never have we been
    apart,
Yet dimensions crossed-
Where only in Lovers hearts can be found,
Passions running wild, unraveling times yet,
Need to be transversed,
You who has freed this soul of mine,
Take care, allow it never troubles to bare,
Cherish it now deeply,
Beside me you shall stand,
My man behind the veil...
SLB

This Takes My Strength Lord,

This takes my strength Lord,
That I must renew through you Your Holy water,
Your heartfelt songs, Your Psalms of love,
Help my heart to heal Heavenly Father,
Help me,
Stop this agony-I beg of you,
This hurt so deep,
How can I pull through?
Yet, somehow, someway,
I pull myself up,
Just for a moment, just for a moment,
My inner self speaks to me,
It is to God I must release my Soul, my pain,
It is only to Him,
Can I dare to go forward-
So I beg, I plead, I pray-
If not whole, at least make me a part,
A small, yet whole part,
That through faith,
The pieces will come together again,
And only through the Will of God,
I step forward, one step and then another,
With the hope, I will not fall,
But go slowly forward, with
The Will of God...
SLB

We Will

We will,
No sphere of existence can separate,
We have gone back in time and saw each other,
We feel the strength when we call for it,
It is real, as real as the truth that made it,
Perish not,
Yet let it blossom to its fullest on this Earth,
And peacefully take us on to our next existence,
Where shall we be as one,
This man and me...
SLB

Signs From the After Life----

I am very pleased to have communication with the after-life any time I can. My dear uncle communicated a message through me as well as a dear friend to tell their families. Some of us are more connected to the other side as we are witnessing the dimensions switching and the veils uplifting...

Touch My Hair And Show Me You Are Still With Me

Touch my hair and show me you are still with me,
Show me signs in my world to give me comfort,
For I look up to the heavens in amazement,
You have time to be with me, you care about my life,
Your love has never lessened, you are always here,
I feel that whisper as sure as I remember your words,
The smell of your scent endlessly as if I needed it,
Bringing me thoughts of you, surrounding me with
      your mist,
You who guide my step, that I am reassured I can walk,
Go forward, and I do,
Moving past the veils which separate,
You send me messages from your home,
So near, I could touch,
I am reassured my strength remains,
For I see you in nature, in my music, and numbers,
It feels my calm, your presence is everlasting,
And seeing bits of the hereafter in pink blossoms
      appearing,
When only two times a year they had appeared before,
And as I look once more upon my feet, as a penny
      appears,
The date coincides with just the information I need,
Messages you send, comfort and love,
Walk beside me and make me a believer,
And blessings to you as well, on the other side...
SLB

It is my sincere thank you that I give to my gentleman that he has connected with me through death. Yes I called him a gentleman because that is exactly what he is, never wanting me ever to worry. The first Christmas he played "Yesterday" knowing I loved that song and "Moon River" two times: the first just after I released balloons to him in the sky over Virginia Beach in honor of him six weeks after his death; it came on in the bar as I was walking back to my room. And the second time at Christmas that same year when I turned the radio on going to church. He has played appropriate songs to me at just the right times. He shows me numbers that line up in sequence to show me that he is near. He leaves pennies that have a certain date on them and flowers that send messages. I am very attuned to these messages having told him previous to his death to send whatever he feels I need at the time and not to worry I will not be frightened. You can still do that to your deceased loved ones just tell them you will not be frightened and wish to hear from them in the afterlife. It brings much comfort.

So People Asked Me

So people asked me for questions,
    Of poems I had written,
Imaginations unjust,
    Satisfaction, take hold-
For as I have written,
    You have read,
Answers come to each differently,
    None told, that be said,
Enjoy, Manifest-
    Each breath you do whisper,
Ask not for my answers,
    To not matter,
Look at them with your reality,
    Not mine,
For all life is interconnected,
    They say as we go,
And messages of love,
    Doth come and go,
So think what you will,
    Don't fret or ponder,
It is both my imagination and reality,
    And to that, I do not utter...
SLB

I returned to Antigua three years after we had seen the awe inspiring beauty and a little more than two years after he had passed from this life. He met me there where the heavens can touch this earth, I felt his presence, and found peace in my solitude.

I Went Back

I went back to the English Harbour,
Where the great Atlantic and the Caribbean meet with
    fury,
The parent showing its strength, to its offspring,
Shirley Heights where the souls in heaven reach down
    to but touch,
Only God in all His glory, could such a place exist,
It was here with the majestic beauty of the cliffs, I saw,
You would appear, as if I could reach out and touch,
Standing in awe of such beauty, we had both witnessed
    before,
As if time had gone backwards,
You had come alive, poising a thousand photos for me
    to cherish,
Holding my hand as we wandered the cliffs,
Our love was still very much alive here,

My memories took me back when you physically stood
    here,
As I remembered that day, it was perfect, not that
    long ago,
The word future was a strong part of the equation,
We had it all, our love surrounded us as in a cocoon,
We had been blessed by the Most High,
Nine months later you left to be with God,
We had seen His glory, and then you left me to live at
    His side,
So I sit, quietly,
Gazing into the people strolling past,
Lovers strolling as we had, hand in hand,
Their destiny not yet certain, yet I do so wish blessings,
For we were indeed given a precious bubble of time,
We lived in a perfect time, though we did not foresee
    the future,
We had been literally dropped into a paradise on Earth,
Given a chance to view a precious preview of heaven to
    come,
And it was here as before, I was with my man,
That perfect day in Shirley Heights, the English
    Harbour, Antigua...
SLB

I look around my world the one I built for myself after his death. I still miss him terribly, but I go on, and I live. Yes I have had relationships and people may question how can that be, do you not feel it's too soon or perhaps you forgot about him. I believe it is an individuals' opinion of what is right and wrong for them. You can be in a relationship and still miss the person in heaven. That is normal. When you are allowed to talk about it to another that is even more healing. My man had been gone two and a half years and on his birthday though I tried not to cry, I happened to wonder upstairs for something, wandered on to his photos and weep and talked to him into the wee hours of the night. I found comfort telling my good friend of the opposite sex what had happened as he related he also has the same experiences with his spouse who had passed on. Let your emotions be, crying can be healing. Special days and times will always bring us joy and a little sorrow. Honor them the best we can and wish them love in heaven. I try my best for him to be proud of me as I truly feel he is.

In writing this book two and a half years after his death I still find myself sad if I allow myself to be. I tried to pretend his birthday did not exist. I said Happy Birthday told my friends, called his brother, had a special dinner to celebrate but I tried to hide my true emotions. I was putting something away and saw his picture that I had hidden to hide the pain. I took the picture and talked to him for two hours into the night with non-ending stream of tears. I do believe even when we feel we have worked through the grief it hits so hard at times, it is best to just allow it to happen. I feel his presence while writing this book and I am sure he would be very proud of me. It's actually Palm Sunday and I was getting ready to go some place but his picture stares at me from my writing materials. Picking it up the love never really left it is in heaven, where God lives. I will always do my best to honor him, all my departed loved ones and first God.

You Will Never Be Away

You will never be away,
Though I cannot hear your words,
Your presence visits me at will,
Easing yourself into my thoughts,
Looking at your photo I remember,
Yes, totally engulfing my emotions,
You are here, and as I slowly turn,
I see glimpses of where you sat, thought,
The whys have turned to acceptance,
Do I ever forget, I chose to not think,
I chose to go on, the only way I can,
Those of us who have been there, know,
You feel their pain, as if it were yours,
A bond is formed, because we know,
Yet so many times when I see that photo,
Take me back to when I didn't know the pain,
Take me back to a non-existent understanding,
For you would be here, in the present not the past,
And this smile would be genuine, not painted,
So I survive, I live, I play,
No one knows the hurt that is opened seeing that
      photo,
So I place it carefully back, covering up the hurt,
Never facing the ultimate truth, because,
You will never be away...
      SLB

I found myself conversing with him in heaven through meditation. This seemed to help although it was very near three years since his passing. I called this:

Talking To Heaven

He said, as if I was in a deep dream state,
I am with you, you are not alone,
You have pondered many things through meditation,
Perhaps it is time, you understand,
For I do, I was not taken from you in punishment,
But in love,
I understand it now,
Everything in God's creation, is His plan,
I had to leave you, for change to come,
You will know,
I am with the rest of the family for you,
My love, life is a series of choices,
Choose love,
I am learning as a student of the Most High,
I was met by your and my loved ones,
I will always be with you,
I send thoughts of love to you through nature,
Life is beautiful where I dwell,
I am here to protect you, as a guide,
It was written before our birth,
In life, I should have said more times,
How much I truly loved you,
I did,
Your tears shall cleanse your soul,
As I hold my hands out to wipe them,
I know you did all you could,
Let quilt never consume your heart,
Where love alone shall live...
SLB

Memorials to Our Loved Ones
(put marks on it from Slovak language)

I believe as do many others in this world that it is of utmost respect we honor our loved ones. My relatives come from Hnusta, Slovakia and it brought tears to my eyes to see how very much these people respect the dead. After church on Sundays they go to the cemetery and take care of the graves and flowers are put on all relatives. No one is forgotten. This takes hours and they are honored to do it. My family while I was growing up used to also do that once a week, I still know where all the graves are located. It was called taking care of the graves and my cousin in Los Angeles still believes to this day it is our duty when she is back in town to honor them as such. I am not familiar with other cultures but I think it is a lovely idea.

We pay tribute to those that have passed on our national holidays such as Veterans day to those gone before us and those with us. It is very respectful to have an American flag hanging in honor of their service. I also have candles on my mantle with a picture and fresh sage for their protection.

The urn if one has ashes can be special to the person it honors. My urn for my loved one is from the Czech Republic trimmed in gold and the finest porcelain flowers in a lovely emerald green hue. It has in addition to his ashes inside an angel and a cross to show devotion and care. He is also at a Veterans cemetery with a simple cross. I will take flowers and a flag and a card I sit beside him when I go to visit.

It was only three months after his death when I was asked to go to a memorial candle lighting service at Christmas. It was called Blue Christmas. It was intended for those who had lost a loved one during the year and didn't know how to get through the holidays. It was certainly for me. Four candles were lit. The first represented our grief, the second was for courage to confront the sorrow, the third represented the memories of the loved one, and the fourth was our love. At the end of the service we were given a candle with the persons' name on it and Blue Christmas. I cherish that simple candle and I hold it with respect in my china cabinet.

It was a great honor for me for him to be asked by the community I live in to be remembered at the memorial honors on Memorial Day eight months after his death. They had the procession of the drummers, the presentation of the colors, invocation, Pledge of Allegiance, National Anthem, salute to the armed forces, roll call of departed comrades accompanied by the living flag tribute and tolling the bell, taps, benediction, retirement of colors, and God Bless America. The minister from our church in our community was one of the organizers and one of his dear friends while he was with us in life. The minister called right after he had passed away and told me he felt he had gone. To me that is one of those moments that will always bring tears to my eyes.

For every individual it is different but if we have a pure and honest intention in our heart to honor and remember them that is what is right for you. In my house I have pictures of some of my departed, flowers, jewelry, crosses, and Bibles. Do what makes you comfortable. It is your loss and you need comfort to be able to live with it.

You can honor your loved ones that have gone before you by thanking them for being in your life and remembering them after they are gone. God appreciates when you honor your ancestors by simply saying a simple thank you. By the simple act of honoring them you are also honoring yourself. You do service for those in heaven when you lead a good life on earth. You may also pray to your ancestors and bless them in heaven. Thank them for giving you all the qualities you possess because you inherited them from the loved ones who have gone before you. Pray to them and give them thanks.

To my dear loved ones who have gone before me,

I a living testament to your life am here on my earthly journey and wish to make you proud of me. Whatever I can do of service to God and His people let me do it in the best way I can. I thank all of my ancestors and family and friends who has gone before me. I bless each and every one of them. I thank each one for caring for me and watching over me in my life on earth. I send all the blessings you send to me back to you in heaven. That our love may be a continuous circle in the magic we call life. This we do pray in the holy name of Jesus Christ. Amen.
SLB

Dear God,
Let me be a servant of yours.
Allow me to be a co-worker in providing joy and happiness,
Fill my heart with your love,
Help me to know inner peace,
Declare to me that I am a clear channel to be as one,
To do this in your holy name,
Give me both opportunities and gratitude, that I may serve,
And please keep my thoughts only of you.
Amen.
SLB

I Am Of Service

I am of service Lord to you,
I feel for those who are suffering, my Lord,
Make me a fisher of men, a servant to you,
When someone asks, allow me to show,
The power of prayer that is ours to partake of,
Let me pray for others, for some dare not ask,
Let me pray for those that do not believe yet,
For Your love is greater than we can imagine,
Enveloping the universe and beyond,
And though we are but a grain of sand,
We are precious and loved by Our Creator, Our God,
Allow me to serve, in whatever way You see for me,
Ever faithful and every humble to My Lord...
SLB

The pleasure of just being...
SLB

Chapter 10

Prayers

Matthew 6:33

But seek ye first the Kingdom of God, and his righteousness; and all these things shall be added unto you.

A Prayer for the Dying and a Special Soul

O most merciful Jesus, lover of souls,
I beseech Thee, by the agony of Thy most Sacred Heart,
and by the sorrows of Thine Immaculate Mother,
wash clean in the Thy Blood the sinners of the whole world
who are to die this day.

Remember most especially the soul I spiritually adopt
with the intention of entrusting him or her to Thy Shepherd's
care:
I beseech Thee for the grace to move this sinner, who is in
danger of going to Hell, to repent. I ask this because of my
trust in Thy great mercy.

If it should please Thy Majesty to send me a suffering
this day
in exchange for the grace I ask of this soul, then, it too,

shall please me very much, and I thank Thee, Most Sweet Jesus, Shepherd and Lover of Souls; I thank Thee for this opportunity to give mercy in thanksgiving for all the mercies Thou hast shown me. Amen.

The Daily Practice of Adopting An Unknown Dying Soul

God's mercy is so abundant that He wants to shower it upon earth. He sent His only Son, Our Lord to redeem sinners at the cost of Calvary. Christ would have died on that Cross to redeem but one soul, yet the One Sacrifice was sufficient for all. Redemption, however, does not suffice for salvation, as St. Paul warns us to work out our salvation "in fear and trembling."

With the great Apostasy predicted by the Apostle to the Gentiles come upon uas in these last days many souls are going to Hell: they either do not know how, or cannot pray for themselves. But Jesus Christ is waiting and now is the acceptable time, if only we, who do believe and do pray would only make it a daily habit of unfathomable charity and mercy, to spiritually adopt an unknown dying sinner, asking God for the grace for that person to repent or ask for mercy in his last moments. As a pledge of our fidelity and trust in Christ's mercy, all we have to do is ask through our prayer offering, perhaps if so moved, to offer the intention of our entire day, or to forego one small pleasure that is licit in exchange, at the very least we should make the intention of bearing one inconvenience that day with more patience than is our usual wont for the repentance of that soul. Amen.

The Miracle Prayer

Lord, Jesus, I come before you, just as I am. I am sorry for my sins, I repent of my sins, please forgive me. In your name, I forgot all others for what they have done against me. I renounce Satan, the evil spirits and all their works. I give you my entire self, Lord Jesus, now and forever. I invite you into my life Jesus, I accept you as my Lord, God, and Savior. Heal me, change me, strengthen me in body, soul, and spirit.

Come Lord Jesus, cover me with your precious blood, and fill me with your Holy Spirit. I love you, Lord Jesus. I praise you Jesus. I thank you Jesus. I shall follow you every day of my life. Amen.

Mary my Mother, Queen of Peace, St. Peregrine, the cancer Saint, all you Angels and Saints please help me. Amen.

This was used at the funeral of Paul Bures my father in law, and I believe it is a lovely Psalm. I dedicate this to his grandchildren: Angela, Paul, Anthony, Suzanne, Annette,

Andrew, Robert, Michael and great-grandchildren: Daniel, Annabelle, Mikyta, and all others to come.

Psalm 118
The Lord's Mercy

O Give thanks unto the Lord; for he is good: because his mercy endureth forever. Let Israel now say, that his mercy endureth forever. Let the house of Aaron now say, that his mercy endureth forever. Let them now that fear the Lord say, that his mercy endureth forever. I called upon the Lord in distress: the Lord answered me, and set me in a large place. The Lord is on my side; I will not fear: what can man do unto me? The Lord taketh my part with them that help me: therefore shall I see my desire upon them that hate me. It is better to trust in the Lord than to put confidences in princes. All nations compassed me about: but in the name of the Lord will I destroy them. They compassed me about; yea, they compassed me about: but in the name of the Lord I will destroy them. They compassed me about like bees; they are quenched as the fire of thorns: for in the name of the Lord I will destroy them. Thou hast thrust sore at me that I might fall: but the Lord helped me. The Lord is my strength and song, and is become my salvation. The voice of rejoicing and salvation is in the tabernacles of the righteous: the right hand of the Lord doeth valiantly. The right hand of the Lord is exalted: the right hand of the Lord doeth valiantly. I shall not die, but live, and declare the works of the Lord. The Lord hath chastened me sore: but he hath not given me over unto death. Open to me the gates of righteousness: I will go into them, and I will praise the Lord: this gate of the Lord, into which the righteous shall enter. I will praise thee: for thou hast heard me, and art become my salvation. The stone which the builders refused is become the head stone of the corner. This is the Lord's doing; it is marvelous in our eyes. This is the day which the Lord hath made; we will rejoice and be glad in it. Save now, I beseech thee, O Lord: O Lord, I beseech thee, send now prosperity. Blessed be he that cometh in the name of the Lord: we have blessed you out of the house of the Lord. God is the Lord, which hath shown us light: bind the sacrifice with cords, even unto the horns of the altar. Thou art my God, and I will praise thee: thou art my God, I will exalt thee. O give thanks unto the Lord; for he is good: for his mercy endureth forever.

Luke 2: 29-32

Lord, now lettest thou thy servant depart in peace, according to thy word: for mine eyes have seen thy salvation, which thou hast prepared before the face of all people; a light to lighten the Gentiles, and the glory of thy people Israel.

Prayer to St. Jude

Most holy Apostle, St. Jude,
faithful servant and friend of Jesus,
the Church honors and invokes you
universally as the patron of hope.
Pray for me when I feel helpless and alone.
Please make use of that particular privilege
given to you, to bring hope and
comfort and help where they are needed most.
Come to my assistance in this great need
that I may receive the consolation
and help in my tribulations and sufferings,
particularly (here make your request).
I praise God with you and all the Saints forever.
I promise, blessed St. Jude,
to be ever mindful of this great favor,
to always honor you as
my special and powerful patron,
and to gratefully encourage devotion to you.
Amen.

Footprints in the Sand

One night I had a dream. I dreamed I was walking along the beach with the Lord and across the sky flashed scenes from my life. For each scene I noticed two sets of footprints in the sand, one belonged to me, and the other to the Lord. When the last scene of my life flashed before us, I looked back to the footprints in the sand and I noticed that many times along the path of my life there was only one set of footprints. I also noticed that it happened at the very lowest and saddest times in my life. This really bothered me and I questioned the Lord about it. "Lord you said that once I decided to follow you, you would walk with me all the way. I have noticed that during the most trouble some times of my life there is only one set of footprints. I do not understand why in times I needed you the most you should leave me." The Lord replied, "My precious, precious child, I love you and I would never, never leave you during times of trial and suffering. When you saw only one set of footprints, it was then that I carried you."-author unknown

The Cross In My Pocket

I carry this cross in my pocket
To remind me of who I can be.
If I take up my cross and follow
Wherever my Savior leads me.

The cross is not there as a token
Or a prize I can brag about.
It's there as a personal reminder
Of something I can't live without.

It reminds me of Jesus my Savior
Who died for me and now lives.
Each day I remember my new life,
And the blessings and gifts He gives.

I carry this cross in my pocket
Along with my money and keys.
I keep it close by to remind me
Of what's most important to me.

This cross also is a reminder
Of the love that I feel in my heart
For all of my fellow believers,
A family of which I'm a part.

So I carry a cross to remind me
That along with my family and home,
I take with me the love of Christ Jesus;
With that I am never alone.
---author unknown

Prayer to the Sacred Heart of Jesus

Oh Lord Jesus Christ, to Your most Sacred Heart I confide this intention (name petition). Only look upon me, then do what your love inspires. Let Your Sacred Heart decide, I count on You. I trust in You. I throw myself on Your mercy. Lord Jesus, You will not fail me.

Sacred Heart of Jesus, I trust in You. Sacred Heart of Jesus. I believe in Your love for me. Sacred Heart of Jesus, Your kingdom come. Sacred Heart of Jesus, I have asked You for many favors, but I earnestly implore this one. Take it, place it in Your open Heart. When the Eternal Father looks upon it. He will see it covered with Your precious blood. It will be no longer my prayer, but Yours, Jesus. Sacred Heart of Jesus, I place my trust in You. Let me not be disappointed. Amen.

Prayer to the Holy Trinity
From Our Lady of Lourdes, France

Glory to the Father,
Who by His Almighty power and love created me,
Making me in the image and likeness of God.

Glory be to the Son,
Who by His Precious Blood delivered me from hell,
And opened for me the gates of heaven.

Glory be to the Holy Spirit,
Who has sanctified me in the Sacrament of Baptism,
And continues to sanctify me,
By the Grace I receive daily from His bounty.

Glory be to the Three adorable Persons of the Holy Trinity,
Now and forever. Amen.

Act of Faith-
A prayer of gratitude towards God and a precious gift of faith
from God

O my God, I firmly believe that you are one God in three
divine persons, Father, Son, and Holy Spirit. I believe that your
divine Son became man and died for our sins, and that He will
come to judge the living and the dead. I believe these and all
the truths which the holy Catholic Church teaches, because in
revealing them you can neither deceive nor be deceived. Amen.

Act of Hope-
This is for spiritual comfort and inspiration from God, and used
as a morning prayer.

O My God, relying on Your almighty power and infinite
mercy and promises, I hope to obtain pardon for my sins, the
help of Your grace, and life Everlasting, through the merits of
Jesus Christ, my Lord and Redeemer. Amen.

Act of Charity-
Charity means Love, pray for unselfish love toward God

O my God, I love Thee above all things, with my whole
heart and soul, because Thou art all-good and worthy of all
love. I love my neighbor as myself for the love of Thee. I forgive
all who have injured me, and ask pardon of all whom I have
injured. Amen.

Prayer to Our Lady of Good Counsel

Most Glorious Virgin, chosen by the Eternal Counsel to
be the Mother of the Eternal Word made flesh, thou art the

treasurer of Divine graces, and the advocate of sinners, I, thy most unworthy servant, have recourse to thee; be thou pleased to be my guide and counselor in this vale of tears. Obtain for me through the Most Precious Blood of thy Divine Son, the forgiveness of my sins, the salvation of my soul, and the means necessary to obtain it. I like manner, obtain for Holy Mother the Church victory over her enemies, and the spread of the kingdom of Jesus Christ upon the whole earth. Amen.

To Our Lady of Fatima
Fatima, Portugal May 13-October 13, 1917
Three shepherd children apparitions-peace in our nation and the world

Queen of the Rosary, sweet Virgin of Fatima, who hast deigned to appear in the land of Portugal and hast brought peace, both interior and exterior, to that once so troubled country, we beg of thee to watch over our dear homeland and to assure its moral and spiritual revival. Bring back peace to all nations of the world, so that all, and our own nation in particular, may be happy to call thee their Queen and the Queen of Peace. Our Lady of the Rosary, pray for our country, Our Lady of Fatima, obtain for all humanity a durable peace. Amen.

Pope John Paul II's Prayer to Our Lady of Lourdes

The Pope said the prayer on August 15, 2004 in Lourdes, France and asked Mary, "be our guide along the paths of this world."

Hail Mary, poor and humble Woman. Blessed be the Most High!

Virgin of hope, dawn of a new era, We join in your song of praise,

To celebrate the Lord's mercy, to proclaim the coming of the

Kingdom and the full liberation of humanity.

Hail Mary, lowly handmaid of the Lord, Glorious Mother of Christ!

Faithful Virgin, holy dwelling-place of the Word, Teach us to preserve

In listening to the Word, and to be docile to the voice of the Spirit,

Attentive to his promptings in the depths of our consciousness and to

His manifestations in the events of history.

Hail Mary, Woman of sorrows, Mother of the living! Virgin spouse

Beneath the Cross, the new Eve, Be our guide along the paths of the world.

Teach us to experience and to spread the love of Christ, to stand with you,

before the innumerable crosses on which your son is still crucified.

Hail Mary, woman of faith, First of the disciples! Virgin Mother of

the Church, help us always to account for the hope that is in us,

with trust in human goodness and the Father's love.

Teach us to build up the world beginning from within:

In the depths of silence and prayer,

In the joy of fraternal love, in the unique fruitfulness of the Cross.

Holy Mary, Mother of believers, Our Lady of Lourdes, pray for us.

Amen.

St. Raphael prayer for healing

Glorious Archangel St. Raphael, great prince of the heavenly court, you are illustrious for your gifts of wisdom and grace. You are a guide of those who journey by land or sea or air, consoler of the afflicted, and a refuge of sinners.

I beg you, assist me in all my needs and in all the sufferings of this life, as once you helped the young Tobias on his travels. Because you are the medicine of God, I humbly pray you to heal the many infirmities of my soul and the ills that afflict my body. I especially ask of you the favor (fill in your request). And the great grace of purity to prepare me to be the temple of the Holy Spirit. Amen.

St. Dymphna, May 15 is the Feast Day
Patron Saint of those suffering Nervous and Mental Afflictions

Lord, our God you graciously chose St. Dymphna as Patroness of those afflicted with mental, emotional, and nervous disorders. She is thus an inspiration and a symbol of charity to the thousands who ask her intercession. Please grant Lord, through the prayers of this pure youthful martyr, relief and consolation to all suffering such trials, and especially for those for whom we pray, (mention those for whom you wish to pray). We beg you, Lord, to hear the prayers of St. Dymphna on our behalf. Grant all those for whom we pray patience in their sufferings and resignation to your divine will. Please fill them with hope, and grant them the relief and cure they so much desire. We ask through Christ-Our Lord who suffered agony in the garden. Amen.

St. John the Baptist, June 24 and August 29 are the Feast days
Patron Saint of Monks, Highway Workers, Converts, Convulsions, Printers, and Tailors
In honor of St. John the Baptist
This prayer has three parts according to his life stages.

First:
O Glorious St. John the Baptist, greatest Prophet among those born of woman,

Although thou was sanctified in thy mother's womb and didst lead a most innocent life, nevertheless it was thy will to retire into the wilderness, there to devote thyself to the · practice of austerity and penance; obtain for us of thy Lord the grace to be wholly detached, at least in our hearts, from earthly goods, and to practice Christian mortification with interior recollection and with the Spirit of Holy prayer.

Our Father, Hail Mary, Glory Be

Second:

O most zealous Apostle who, without working any miracles on others, but solely by the example of thy life of penance and the power of thy word, didst draw after thee the multitudes, in order to dispose them to receive the Messiah, worthily and to listen to His heavenly doctrine; grant that it may be given unto us, by means of that example of a holy life and the exercise of every good work, to bring souls to God, but above all those souls that are enveloped in the darkness bring of error and ignorance and are led astray by vice.

Our Father, Hail Mary, Glory Be

Third:

O martyr invincible, who, for the honor of God and the salvation of souls didst with firmness and constancy withstand the impiety of Herod even at the cost of thine own life, and didst rebuke him for his wicked and dissolute life; by thy prayers obtain for us a heart, brave and generous, in order that we may overcome all human respect and openly profess our faith in loyal obedience to the teachings of Jesus Christ, Our Divine Master.

Our Father, Hail Mary, Glory Be

Pray for us St. John the Baptist, that we may be worthy of the promises of Christ. Amen.

Prayer for The Seven Gifts of the Holy Spirit

O Lord Jesus Christ, Who, before ascending into heaven, didst promise to send the Holy Ghost to finish thy work in the souls of Thy Apostles and Disciples, deign to grant the same Holy Spirit to me, that He may perfect in my soul the work of Thy grace and Thy love. Grant me the Spirit of Wisdom that I may despise the perishable things of this world and aspire only after the things that are eternal. The Spirit of Understanding to enlighten my mind with the light of Thy divine truth, the Spirit of Counsel that I may ever choose the surest way of pleasing God and gaining Heaven, the Spirit of Fortitude that I may bear my cross with Thee, and that I may overcome with courage all the obstacles that oppose my salvation, the Spirit of Knowledge that I may know God and know myself and grow perfect in the science of the Saints, the Spirit of Piety that I may find the service of God sweet and amiable, the Spirit of Fear that I may be filled with a loving reverence towards God, and may dread in any way to displease Him. Mark me, dear Lord, with the sign of Thy true disciples and animate me in all things with Thy Spirit. Amen.

There is also a Novena to The Seven Gifts of The Holy Spirit which is begun during the 7th week of Easter. It is the oldest Novena and thought to be written by the Lord himself.

I would recommend reciting it, in all its glory. God Bless.

Prayer for Grace

O My God and My All, in Thy goodness and mercy, grant that before I die I may regain all the graces which I have lost through my carelessness and folly.

Permit me to attain the degree of merit and perfection to which Thou didst desire to lead me, and which I failed by my unfaithfulness to reach.

Mercifully grant also that others regain the graces which they have lost through my fault. This I humbly beg through the merits of the Sacred Heart of Jesus and Immaculate Virgin Mary. Amen.

Litany of Saint Michael of the Saints

Lord have mercy on us,	Christ, graciously hear us,
Christ have mercy on us,	have mercy on us,

Lord have mercy on us,	have mercy on us,
Christ, hear us,	have mercy on us,
God, the Father of Heaven,	have mercy on us,
God the Son, Redeemer of the World,	have mercy on us,
God, the Holy Spirit,	have mercy on us,
Holy Trinity, one God, Father, Son, and Holy Spirit	have mercy on us,
Michael, child of God,	pray for us,
Servant of Jesus Christ,	pray for us,
Companion of Mary,	pray for us,
Spiritual Innocence,	pray for us,
Mystical Heart,	pray for us,
Soul enamored of God	pray for us,
Friend of the poor,	pray for us,
Patron of the cancer stricken,	pray for us,
Model of charity,	pray for us,
Model of sanctity,	pray for us,
Light of those in doubt,	pray for us,
Lover of the Holy Spirit,	pray for us,
Helper of the Needy,	pray for us,
Slave of divine love,	pray for us,
Hope of those who trust in you,	pray for us,
Inspiration of pastors and priests,	pray for us,
Lamb of God, Who takes away the sins of the World,	spare us, O Lord

Lamb of God, Who takes away   graciously hear us, O Lord,
the sins of the World,

Lamb of God, Who takes away   have mercy on us,
the sins of the World,

Pray for us Saint Michael of
the Saints,

That we may be made worthy   Amen.
of the promises of Christ.

 I found a beautiful Novena to Jesus. It is a nine day Novena; however because of copyright, I can just recommend it. I found it on the internet. Our life is easier now with the internet, and I would suggest looking at this lovely Novena to Jesus.

 Prayers are way of communicating to the One Who holds us all...
SLB

Conclusion:

To the one who inspired this book may I say, our relationship continues for the veils of our existence to the next are growing smaller, and the ones on the other side are capable of being in more than one place at a time, and able to help us if we give them permission to do it, otherwise free will, won't permit it.

God's love is a miracle. Always put God first and believe we are saved. I hope you all find your miracle. I hope Our Lord Jesus Christ be with you in heart, mind, and spirit and lead you on your journey, as He alone led me. In God's greatest love to all mankind, go serve the Lord and Live in Peace...

Write Your Thoughts About Hospice

Printed in the United States
By Bookmasters